INTRODUCTION

Captovation
Online Presentations by Design

Scott J. Allen, Ph.D.
Maria Soriano Young

Captovation
Online Presentations by Design

Copyright © 2020 Scott J. Allen & Maria Soriano Young

All rights reserved. Printed in the United States of America. No part of this book may be used or reproduced in any manner whatsoever without written permission except in the case of brief quotations embodied in critical articles and reviews. For contact information visit www.captovation.ai.

ISBN-13: 978-1-7358704-3-4

Cover design by: Scott Taylor, BlkDog

First Edition

Dedication

Scott dedicates this book to Larry Morrow—an inspirational teacher, mentor, and friend.

Maria dedicates this book to her husband, David, and her parents, Ben and Joni, who have always supported and encouraged her as a writer, teacher, and presenter; she also dedicates this book to her aunt Geri Deane, who she has looked up to as a role model of professionalism and kindness to others for many years.

Foreword

Where were you in March 2020 when the world shut down? There was a Darwinian pressure thrust upon many of us: adapt or die. A time to re-evaluate, a time to reflect, a time to evolve. Survival became the new success.

The COVID-19 coronavirus pandemic forced countless event cancellations, the service/hospitality industry shut down, planes were grounded, and borders were closed. Through the cancellations and postponements, people understood that the show must go on—even if that "show" looked dramatically different than what we were accustomed to. A new horizon of communication practices has appeared…

Enter virtual gatherings and meetings.

The pandemic has led to new global standards for working—especially from home. Digital productivity has transformed all around us, no matter where you choose to work.

There's been a dramatic increase in usage of online platforms such as Zoom, WebEx, and Teams. And along with the increase in platforms comes your need to excel in this new medium.

How do you make sure you hit it out of the park, even if you are sitting on your bed in your comfy socks? Or a suit and tie, dialed in from the waist up?

Thank goodness for Scott Allen and Maria Soriano Young.

They decided to commit to research and author a remarkable book to help us navigate these challenging times. Their offering is steeped in practicality and truth. A matter-of-fact, pragmatic approach to coaching all of us up to be the best we can be. It is desperately needed because there's often less accountability with online gatherings.

I once made a sandwich, responded to 10+ emails, read an article in the *Times*, and did a puzzle with my kid, all while "watching" a 90-minute online presentation. I'm not proud of it, but I know I'm not alone. You know you are in trouble as a presenter when an audience member defaults to a thumbnail picture or chooses not to activate their video screen.

It's not a giant leap to conclude that similar behaviors extend to web audiences, where the cloak of invisibility and easy access to multiple devices invite the opportunity to escape.

Understanding how to keep your audience engaged, and working with the challenges of the medium and the technology, requires some strategic but necessary adjustments in the design and delivery of your online presentation.

Use the methodology, tips, and tricks in this book, and you will have no problem creating high-impact virtual presentations. Go through these ideas every time you have a presentation to make, and you will soon find your peers and associates turning to you for assistance when it comes to creating a virtual presentation—one that is captivating and meaningful.

This pressure is good for us.

Evolve with it.

It will be easier for you if you implement what is in this book.

David Rae
President & Co-Founder / 503 Creative
Curator / TEDxPortland

Acknowledgments

We acknowledge with deep gratitude all those who we interviewed during the research phases of our project. Our Zoom and email conversations with all of you were enlightening and informative, and your experiences and contributions greatly expand the dimensions of our text. In addition, we are thankful that our interview opportunities allowed us to strengthen existing connections, as well as forming new ones. Thank you to the following people:

- Aaron Beverly, 2019 Toastmasters World Champion of Public Speaking
- Micki Byrnes, President & General Manager at WKYC-TV
- Christina Cashin, Senior Vice President of Talent Management at KeyBank
- Brandon Charpied, Executive Director of the Management & Organizational Behavior Teaching Society
- Jennifer Cowles, Leader of Leadership and Executive Programs at KeyBank
- Ryan Franks, Business Manager at Energy Storage Response Group
- Karen Gilliam, Agency Chief Learning Officer & OD Capability Lead at NASA
- Marc Gillinov, MD, Chair of the Department of Thoracic & Cardiovascular Surgery at Cleveland Clinic
- Ed Markey, Vice President of Corporate Communications at Goodyear Tire & Rubber Co.
- Maggie Mills and Sasha Haines, National Champions of Public Forum Debate, Speech and Debate Association (2020)
- Ty McTigue, Director of Enterprise Solution Sales, Acuity Brands
- Larry Oskowski, National Sales Senior Director at GOJO Industries
- Lillian Powell, Accountant at Defense Finance and Accounting Service
- David Rae, President/Co-Founder of 503 Media & Events and founder of TEDxPortland
- Eileen Sheil, Vice President of Communications at Medtronic
- Scott Taylor, Owner & Creative Director at BlkDog
- Andrew Ziemba, Program & Licensing Manager at MTD Products

We also want to thank our reviewers for taking the time out of their own busy lives to read the text and provide both endorsements and critical feedback. Thank you to Marshall Goldsmith, Dr. Mary Ellen Guffey, Gordon Daily, Abby McNutt, Ken Kasee, and Deepak Menon for their praise and faith in our work; to the students of Scott Allen's Executive Communication course at John Carroll University for their "test read" of the text and their comments; and to Gabriela Wanless, who dedicated additional time to proofread our work and give us specific suggestions.

Special thanks to Justin Grammens, co-founder of Captovation and the architect of the technology that accompanies this book.

Finally, we want to express our gratitude to Scott Taylor, Owner & Creative Director at BlkDog, who assisted with all of the visual design work for this text—including the cover art, diagrams, and tables.

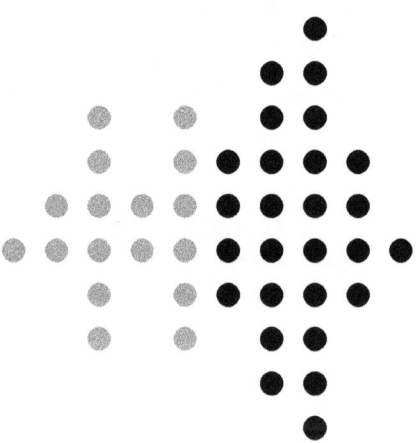

Table of Contents

Introduction 11

Chapter 1: Audience-Centered Design 21

Chapter 2: Design Your Structure 43

Chapter 3: Design Your Visuals 59

Chapter 4: Design Your Setting and Tech 77

Chapter 5: Design Your Delivery 91

Chapter 6: Design For Continual Growth 123

Chapter 7: Design Your Participation 135

Conclusion 145

Appendix 148

About the Authors 158

Praise for Captovation 160

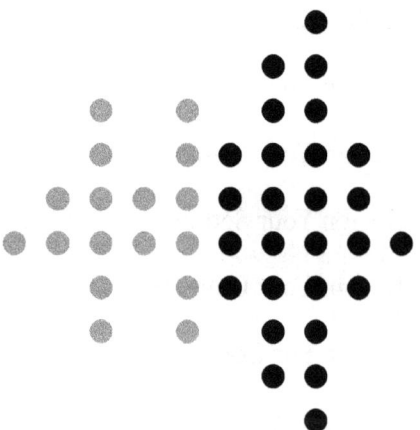

INTRODUCTION

"What did you learn today? What mistake did you make that taught you something? What did you try hard at today?"
—Carol Dweck, *Mindset*

We would venture to guess that most of you had never heard of Microsoft Teams, Zoom, Google Meet, or any of the other major video conferencing platforms that are common household names prior to March 2020. We'd also wager that the vast majority of you had never attended a virtual happy hour, a virtual sales call, a virtual retreat, or conference hosted completely online—nor would you have chosen to do so if there were online and in-person options. We get it; we wouldn't have chosen to attend any of those events online either, and even now, we still may prefer to meet and talk with other people in person. What we do know is that both inside and outside the world of work, it's likely that we will look back on 2020 as the moment that so many elements of our lives changed. What this means is that for some, remote work will become the norm. For others, sales presentations will no longer involve extensive travel—rather, they will occur online. And as virtual teams continue to become the normal way that employees and clients will work together, retreats, meetings, and planning sessions will no longer need to occur face-to-face. For financial reasons and to preserve the health and safety of others, we'll be required to spend most of our days in front of a screen.

In some ways, the shifts mentioned above are positive. For some, online work may allow for a better work/life balance or may reduce travel time. In other cases, these changes could reduce expenses for both companies and individuals, and could create efficiencies and opportunities never imagined. In reality, the new landscape of work represents a great deal of opportunity for many organizations to refocus, reimagine, and reinvent.

With the positives have also come challenges, and there's been a steep learning curve on multiple fronts. We've witnessed high-level executives show up as befuddled and ill-prepared and have seen some well-respected colleagues perform presentations in what looked to be poorly lit closets. Perhaps worse are the cheesy digital backgrounds that render the individual a ghostly figure as they move in and out of focus (despite the humor that comes along with seeing a colleague virtually sitting in the middle of a baseball stadium). As we settle into this new mode of working and communicating, we would guess there will be fewer instances of cats walking across screens, glitchy tech, and awkward camera angles! And maybe, just maybe, we will hear, "Carl, I think you are on mute" less and less as time goes on.

We believe that this is the first comprehensive resource about online presentations that explores the subtle nuances of delivery that may not immediately come to mind, especially as we challenge you to take a more active stance by *thoughtfully designing* each aspect of that presentation. If you are reading this book, you are undoubtedly familiar with the traditional norms and best practices of effective presentations. Rest assured, the foundational concepts are still in place, so that means you already have a baseline for creating and delivering successful presentations online.

However, there are some subtle (but important) shifts in this new medium. Maggie Mills, 2020 National Champion in the Public Forum Debate of the National Speech and Debate Association, said it well when she told us, "I think that all of the weaknesses that exist in live debate are magnified by Zoom. I think that's true of most presentations I've seen. If you don't have good eye contact in person, it's unlikely that you're going to be making eye contact with the webcam." We agree, and have also seen in our experiences that everything is amplified with an online presentation. The good news is that each of us can improve, develop, and grow. After all, this medium is just different and it's going to take deliberate practice to become an expert.

The future of presentations is here, ready or not. We feel that 2020 will forever be marked as the date when work shifted, education shifted, life shifted; in other words, the year of *creative disruption*. And even though conferences, meetings, and workshops may return to being offered in-person eventually, we strongly believe that a "web option" will remain prominent. This notion is echoed by Brandon Charpied, Executive Director of the Management & Organizational Behavior

Teaching Society, who said, "The fact that we must all come to terms with is that online learning will not be going away following the pandemic. It will undoubtedly be scaled back, but it will remain here to stay."

Why "Captovation"?

We have one goal with this book—to build confidence. More specifically, we want to build *your* confidence. Your confidence in delivering captivating online presentations that help you close the deal, win hearts, secure funding, inspire change, and change the world. So what is Captovation? Two words that translate to "attract" (captivate) and "applause" (ovation). We believe that this book will accelerate your journey toward attracting (digital) applause on your path to accomplishing your goals.

A second reason for the term "Captovation" is because it's the name of a technology platform that can be used alongside the book to accelerate your development and growth. The technology is emerging, but like many other dimensions, we are exploring how technology can help you feel more confident, improve more rapidly, and augment human coaching. For more information on this dimension of the learning process, visit www.captovation.ai.

Our Emphasis on "Design"

> *"A designer knows he or she has achieved perfection not when there is nothing left to add, but when there is nothing left to take away."*
> —Antoine de Saint-Exupery

Our use of the word "design" in the title of this book, and throughout the sections, is an intentional choice because of its complex nature and its mental and physical components. Architects design buildings. Scientists design experiments. Computer scientists designed the computer, phone, or tablet you are using to read this book. Thus, we view the topic of delivering engaging online presentations, in part, as a design challenge.

Why?

- You *design* the structure and central message of your talk.
- You *design* your slide deck.
- You *design* a masterful delivery.
- You *design* your setting and space.
- You *design* your plan for growth and development.

It's not a stretch to imagine that each of you reading this book has found yourself viewing an ineffective online presentation in recent months. The question is, *why* was it boring, demotivating, or ineffective? While we cannot answer for every poor presenter you saw, we would assert that there was a design challenge somewhere in that process.

Throughout this book, we will consistently return to this notion of design—both in terms of the mental exercise it requires and its active, hands-on connotations. What we mean by that is, design requires intentionality, a plan, forethought, and a purpose or desired end-state. It also requires time, emotions, tools, an eraser or the "delete" button, investment, and persistence. *Great* design requires creativity and nudges the world forward. And for you, that means activity, practice, and engagement.

Design is also a process that takes time and investment, and involves some kind of tactile element—whether that means physically sketching out the details of a Prezi before putting together the presentation (like Maria does) or moving graphical parts around a computer screen. We encourage you to stop after you read a section of our book and try something, or test it out—for example, if you're sitting at your normal workspace and reading this book, stop momentarily after you read the section about your background and setting. Open up your Microsoft Teams, Zoom, Google Meet, or other online meeting platform, and look around at everything *except* yourself. What's in that background... maybe that you didn't realize before? This type of reactionary approach is exactly what we are hoping for you to gain from this book, and represents the intentional approach that we want you take as you become a more conscious designer of your presentations (or your participation as an audience member).

Ultimately, we are excited to help you design online presentations that cause people to say:

- She was incredible!
- She was so well-prepared!
- That slide deck was awesome!
- I need to tell others about him.
- He was really good.
- I am so happy I attended.
- That person is going places. Wow!
- They are going to go far!
- I want to contact that person afterward and tell them how meaningful that talk was.

Our Research

Delivering online presentations is a quickly-emerging topic with little to no academic literature base that we have located. The landscape is forming as you read this text, and in a sense, we are learning in real-time. However, we believe that many fundamentals (e.g., use of voice, gestures, effective slide design, and sound structure) remain important; however, each of these brings nuances and adjustments in an online environment.

Our approach to researching this book is fourfold. First, we have looked at the literature for clues. We assume that topics related to general presentation skills that have a substantive literature base, such as respecting time boundaries, effective use of pitch, and signposting, hold in an online environment. We share many of those results here, and many other tried and true topics, but seek as our primary objective to explore the nuances of an online environment. Our second approach to the research was to interview senior-level executives, national champion debaters, and a world champion speaker about the transition. Many themes emerged from these conversations, and have informed the content of this book. You will also find poignant quotes from some of these interviewees throughout. The third component of our work was to conduct two informal surveys on social media platforms to take the pulse of business professionals. The first survey was geared toward anyone who had been a participant in an online meeting over the past few months, and asked respondents to rate the importance of a variety of attributes of online presentations. The second was aimed at managers, to ask about their expectations of their employees when attending or presenting to them. More rigorous research will be conducted in the coming months and years, but it was interesting to capture a snapshot just a few months into the transition. The final aspect that has informed this book is our own experience. Scott has taught and consulted on the topic of presentation skills for more than a decade. In addition to her work as an editor, author, and work as a writing coach, Maria taught the business communications courses at our university.

Mindset/Skillset

The first step in learning how to create more effective online presentations, and to elicit some of the sentiments we listed above, is to accept the reality that this is what you, your colleagues, your bosses, and most other people in your industry are just going to *have to do*. In other words, we hope that you will approach this guide with a positive mindset and are willing to try and to learn!

Carol Dweck[1] has advanced the notion of mindset in recent years. In her work, she spends a lot of time differentiating between a growth mindset and a fixed mindset as a way to emphasize the allowances of a growth mindset. An individual with a fixed mindset shuts down the notion that they can improve, develop, and grow. When it comes to the topic of presentation skills, it is common for people to make remarks like, "Well, I'm just not good at presenting," "I will never feel completely comfortable in front of others," "I am not a charismatic or funny presenter," and so on. These perspectives lock the speaker into a certain way of being and suggest that they do not believe that they will improve (because they don't want to).

When Scott is coaching someone and that person says, "I am not good at commanding the room" he responds with, "*yet*," as if to simply add onto the sentence and to point out that the presenter's mindset is locking them into a certain reality. Why is that additional word so poignant? *Because it changes the conversation.*

In her TED Talk, *The Power of Believing That You Can Improve*, Dweck introduces a powerful idea: the concept of "yet."[2] The sentiment of a statement can shift from representing a fixed mindset to a growth mindset if a speaker includes the word "yet" at the end of the phrase. Thus, adding the word "yet" keeps people in a place of exploration and growth, as opposed to a place of fixed reality. According to Dweck, people with a growth mindset see room for improvement, stay in the game, and see failure and setbacks as an opportunity to grow. They see themselves on a continuum of development versus a fixed place.

The lesson here is to pay close attention to the inner chatter that consumes your mind. As a presenter, do you view setbacks as cold realities or opportunities to learn? Are you overly critical if a presentation did not go as well as you had hoped, or do you capture the learning experience and move on? Do you jump into new and novel situations, or do you sit back and keep safe? Presenters with a growth mindset:

- believe they can get better at their craft
- enjoy the process of improving
- do not set unrealistic expectations for themselves
- understand the power of the word "yet"
- do not let setbacks define who they are
- love a good challenge
- view feedback and constructive criticism positively

Placing yourself on the fixed to growth mindset continuum at the beginning of your learning process as you enter this book is critical—not just for you, but for anyone hoping to improve their presentation skills. It's important to continually monitor your own self-talk and reflect on how your mindset shapes your behavior. So, no, you may not feel like you are the strongest online presenter...**yet**...but by accepting the challenge of learning through this book and by willingly adopting a growth mindset, we are confident that you will get there.

Delivering Online Presentations—The Big Five

Online presentations present challenges and opportunities. The primary difficulties revolve around technology and audience engagement. The good news is that both can be managed with careful thought and preparation.

While it can be difficult to even get *experts* to agree on the characteristics of an excellent live presentation, and when informal poll results reveal a scattered opinion of "what matters most," we are going to explore the main points in this text.[3] When *we* think of great online presentations, there are some core elements of engagement that we want you to focus on. Presenting online requires *you* to be really good at capturing the listener's attention. There are several distractions you are competing with, and in our experience, there are some critical elements of great online presentations. These high-ticket items should be areas of focus as you practice and perform. While we mention these five concepts briefly right now, we will spend more time developing them later on and throughout this text. But as you read, keep these central principles in mind.

Oral Signposts & Clean Structure

Oral signposts help listeners follow the trajectory of your presentation. They are clues that guide listeners through the narrative. Phrases like "my agenda for today" or "the outline of my talk" provide listeners with your overall path.

Repetition

Similar to oral signposts, repetition is a rhetorical technique designed to facilitate recall and retention of your content. To be clear, repetition can be disastrous and unconscious, and what we are really referring to here is the repeated mention of the same words, phrases, images, or even data numerous times throughout your presentation.

This is not what we are advocating. Quite the opposite—we suggest that carefully placed and intentional use of repetition is a powerful tool, especially if you want engagement. The Greeks identified many strategies of repetition, which are highlighted in the article *Effective Rhetorical Strategies of Repetition*.[4]

Vocal Variety

The concept is simple in theory, but difficult to master in practice. In short, vocal variety underpins great storytelling and serves as an opportunity to *use* variations in pitch, pause, tone, pace, and volume to engage listeners. Effective vocal variety breathes life into your presentation and keeps listeners engaged—and if you are outstanding, enthralled.

Word Choice

Presenting online requires you, the presenter, to create the energy. Part of this is done via vocal variety, but we suggest that word choice is another critical element of engagement. Using words that communicate wonder, excitement, frustration, or gratitude will engage listeners in ways that correspond with what emotions you aim to elicit. One caveat is that your nonverbals must align with your words—this is called congruence. For instance, the phrase "I'm excited" often requires a smile to be congruent.

Multimodality

Christina Cashin, the Senior Vice President of Talent Management at KeyBank, reminded us that online presenters should "use a lot of different tools and techniques to pull the audience in." Her assertion was one of many similar sentiments shared by the people we interviewed. We use the term "multimodality" to communicate the need to "switch things up" and not default into one mode (often lecture) for extended periods of time. As we will discuss in more detail later, adding a poll, a question in the chat, or sharing a quick video are ways to facilitate engagement.

Conclusion—An Analog Topic With a Digital Twist

"The goal of effective communication should be for listeners to say 'Me too!' versus 'So what?'"
—Jim Rohn, speaker

There are hundreds, if not thousands of books on the topic of presentation skills. However, we have not found any specifically designed (there's that word again) for the online environment. This reality presents a wonderful opportunity for us as authors, and for you as a reader. We believe that with some conscious practice and attention, you can quickly set yourself apart from the competition in this new and emerging medium.

While many of the topics are the same (e.g., the importance of structure and slide design), many of the traditional topics have nuances online, such as eye contact, hand gestures, and participation. You will find as you read this book that while many of the skills necessary for good presentations in person also apply online, there are some significant (and additional) differences between the two spaces; we applaud you for taking the time to explore this new domain with us.

As you read, observe, and practice, we would love to hear from you. What have we missed? What subtle differences are you noticing? What topics would you like us to address? What research would you like us to conduct? We are open to your suggestions and look forward to your feedback.

CHAPTER 1:
AUDIENCE-CENTERED DESIGN

"You must have an appreciation for what the audience experiences as you use the technology."

—Ed Markey, Vice President of Corporate Communications at Goodyear Tire & Rubber Co.

Before you begin conceptualizing and planning your presentation, it's critical to ensure that you understand your audience and have a clear understanding of their expectations. Without this information, you are guessing, which is not a recipe for success. As a result, there are some critical questions to ask (either to yourself or to a contact at the organization who can give you more information) as you design your presentation.

First, consider or find out about the people themselves—those to whom you will be speaking. Since you will see their faces, hear their voices, and see their comments in the chat box, you want to think about what they expect from you and what you can expect from them during the pre-design phase. Here are some questions to consider about your audience:

- How many people will be tuning in?
- Will they be on individual devices, or will they be gathered in one room?
- Will participants be mobile, at home, or at their desks?
- What devices might they be using?
- When and where will my audience be accessing this content? Will they be tuning in live, watching a recording later, or both?
- Will participants remain on mute?
- Will participants be expected to have their screens on?

In addition to the attendees themselves and their expectations, there are norms around technology and flow that must be clarified before you can begin the design process. Micki Byrnes, President & General Manager at WKYC-TV, told us the following: "However you decide to do the chat protocol, figure it out. Stick with it, and let everybody know at the top of the presentation." Consistency with your strategies is critical so that audiences can focus on what you are saying and what they want to say when they engage, not worrying about *how* to engage. While not an exhaustive list, here are some of the significant questions to clarify before designing your session.

- What platform will we be using (you'd want to know this in advance in case you need to downloadand familiarize yourself with a new platform)?
- What is the general flow of our time together?
- What are the time boundaries for my portion? The Q & A?
- Who will provide introductions (i.e., will the meeting host introduce you, or will you have the opportunity to introduce yourself)?
- Is this audience familiar with the technology? Do they need a tour of the functionalities?
- Could I project an opening slide or a scrolling slideshow while participants are signing in, or would you prefer to begin with a blank screen or faces showing?
- Will questions be asked via the chat functions?
- How will the Q & A segment work? Will people ask throughout or after?
- Will participants with questions raise their hands?
- Will all functionalities be available (e.g., polls, breakout rooms)?
- What is the appropriate dress code?

Once you gain some background information about your audience members, the technology, and the flow, you can then start to think about the content of your presentation and its elements (slides, handouts, etc.). You'll want to get a sense of what the organization expects from the content and format of your presentation before you start creating your slides. Recently, Scott worked with a CEO who prefers "PowerPoint Lite"—in other words, that CEO does not want presenters to come to him with long slide decks full of text. While this might be a preference for some organizations, in other contexts, the expectation is that you cram as much content as possible on the slide.

Thus, a clear understanding of the norms and expectations is critical as you design your presentation. Some questions in the phase may include:

- Is there content I must include?
- Are there limits on the number of slides or amount of text on each slide?
- Do members of the audience have expectations I should understand?
- Will participants have a strong command of the content?

- What does the audience already know? What do they need to know?
- What can I do to make the vast majority of audience members feel content?

Extreme Clarity of Purpose

> *"A wise man speaks because he has something to say; a fool because he has to say something."*
> —Plato, philosopher

When we are designing presentations (whether for professionals, students, or conference attendees), we think about audience members at home after the event has concluded. We envision them speaking with their family or roommates and debriefing the day. Inevitably, they will be asked the question, "How was your session?" This is a critical question, and in some ways, it's the ultimate test of your success. Do those audience members say, "It was incredible, you know…" or is it more of a "Meh. I wish I'd had my morning back"?

You need to base your presentation on its purpose—why, more specifically, you are presenting that day. Presumably, the purpose has been articulated in your conversations with the organization or person who has invited you to speak; if you're not clear on that, you'll want to ask more specifically. The purpose will help you decide on the most appropriate tone, emotion, and vocabulary.

Clear Learning Objectives

Based on how you'd want your audience members to respond, here are some questions you can consider during the design phase:

What do you want them to learn? After the presentation ends (whether 10 minutes or 10 days later), can the audience member accurately reiterate the important content you wanted them to know? Or is it lost in a haze of content and missed opportunity? All too often, a presenter will throw the "kitchen sink" at their audience, hoping that some will stick: too much data and text, every angle and fact to consider, and graphics galore. This results in audience members who are overwhelmed and exhausted, and they will tune out quickly. When asked about the presentation, their responses will be something like "I don't know what was most important to remember...there was too much information." To avoid overwhelming your audience members, begin by asking yourself: What are the few facts, ideas, or concepts you want your audience to recall?

How do you want them to feel? In the same hypothetical conversation, the individual sharing their day will have an emotional response embedded in their answer. How people feel at the end of your presentation is almost as important as what they know.

What do you want them to do? Another design challenge to think about ahead of time is complete clarity on what you want the audience to do with their newly found knowledge and enthusiasm. Do you want them to donate time, talent, or treasure? Rethink their stance on an issue? Even if there is not a concrete action you have in mind, you may simply be seeking their support. Changing human behavior based on your ability to emotionally move them to do so is an incredibly powerful skill.

Based on the hypothetical objectives noted above, next time you are designing a session, be sure to think about the *learn*, *feel*, and *do*. Can they tell someone else (a coworker who had to step away from the presentation for a moment, their boss, or their significant other) your key points? Do they feel excited and enthused about your product, service, or idea? And, perhaps most importantly, are they willing to change their behavior (invest, vote, advocate, support) based on their time with you?

Based on the information you receive in the initial contract meeting, you have a lot to think about. In addition to clarity of purpose, you hopefully will also have clear objectives at this point. These should be agreed upon by you and your contact, and it's also useful for you to present these to your audience at either the beginning or the end of the presentation (or both). Some examples include:

- At the end of the presentation, participants will understand the importance of digital marketing.

- At the end of the presentation, participants will have a clear understanding of the eight largest social media platforms and their functionalities.
- At the end of the presentation, participants will understand and feel enthusiastic about the opportunities afforded by digital marketing techniques.

Once you are clear on the audience and what you want them to *learn, feel,* and *do* (your purpose), as well as your specific learning objectives, you can begin the hands-on process of designing the experience. While the following section may feel overwhelming at first glance, each element is critical if you are serious about designing a transformational learning experience.

Presentation Design

> *"90% of how well the talk will go is determined before the speaker steps on the platform."*
> —Somers White, speaker

Design for Multiple Entry Points

As you begin the design process, be mindful of the various devices and screen sizes a remote audience might be tuning in on; a person tuning in on their cell phone will be viewing the presentation in a different way than someone who is watching on a full-size desktop monitor. We have had attendees access our presentations on tablets, laptops, personal computers, and cell phones. In some cases, attendees were not using the video—instead, they were accessing the presentation as a phone call. Understanding *how* people will log in and engage with the presentation and maintaining awareness that your participants' access points *could* be all of the above is an important consideration as you design.

Design for Stickiness

Because participants will be experiencing your presentation in so many different ways, it's important, if possible, to send your materials ahead of time. Doing so will better prepare the individual who is "on the go" and not in front of their desktop. Likewise, participants will have time to prepare and reflect upon the content. Another design tool for ensuring your message is remembered is the rhetorical technique of repetition. If they are hearing some elements of your content 2–3 times, they are more likely to recall your central message. Likewise, remember the "power of three." If you can package your main points in a way that sticks, participants will more likely recall your content. Here are some common phrases that exemplify our point:

- "Reduce, reuse, recycle."
- "People, planet, profit."
- "Life, liberty, and the pursuit of happiness."
- "...of the people, by the people, for the people."
- "Stop, drop, and roll."
- "Location, location, location!"

A fourth technique is to keep your slide design simple and clean. We have two quotes to keep in mind as you design your slide decks. The first is attributed to Blaise Pascal, who said, "If I had more time, I would have written a shorter letter." The second quote is from Apple co-founder Steve Jobs, who stated that "Simple can be harder than complex: You have to work hard to get your thinking clean to make it simple." Nobody wants excessive clutter, unreadable charts, and confusing graphics. Take the time to get your thinking clean, eliminate noise, add strong visuals, and tell stories that align with your purpose.

Designing for Time

One executive we recently spoke with shared how time (as a concept) has significantly shifted in his line of business. He lamented that his team used to have much more time with clients and now, they are often relegated to a 30-minute online meeting. Christina Cashin, the Senior Vice President of Talent Management at KeyBank, also observed this shift. She is used to designing full-day programs and after the extreme move to a work-from-home culture, she told us, "For me, it has to be short and engaging—like 60 minutes. Ninety minutes is pushing it and anything past 90 minutes, I just start to zone out, or multitask, or get distracted. So to me, the norm should be shorter content, maybe more frequently." What used to be a full or half-day session is now significantly reduced or spread over a period of weeks. What this suggests for you as a designer is that you may need to significantly alter what you would have done before, perhaps into a shorter amount of time, or into different increments. While we highlighted only a couple examples in this paragraph, it's important to note that shifts in how we approach time emerged a common theme among the executives we interviewed—therefore, it is a crucial principle to keep in mind.

Another aspect of time is how you, the presenter, use that time in the context of the presentation. Some research has shown that the average attention span for a lecture-based presentation begins to decline at about 10 minutes,[5] while other scholars found that "Students report attention lapses as early as the first 30 seconds of a lecture, with the next lapse occurring approximately 4.5 min into a lecture and again at shorter and shorter cycles throughout the lecture segment."[6] And while there is no conclusive evidence, multiple studies land in the range between 5–20 minutes.[7] All of this suggests that you need to intentionally plan how you will recapture your audience's interest about every 10 minutes. This research was reinforced by Jennifer Cowles, Leader of Leadership and Executive Programs at KeyBank, when she suggested that "You can't go any more than five, seven minutes without having to change the way that people are interacting with you." In the context of a live presentation, this may mean that a participant is simply daydreaming, checking their phone, or engaging in a side conversation. Online, people can "check out" much more easily, which means that you need to be that much better at commanding their attention. Online participants are pulled in multiple directions—sometimes by choice, other times by necessity. In reality, you are competing with their family members, email, project work, personal correspondences, the news, and so on. And they could be doing a variety of activities, from checking and responding to emails to preparing and eating a meal.

Though you cannot control what your audience members actually do during an online presentation, you still want to find ways to get them to turn their attention back to you—to *tune back in*. To avoid the 10-minute fade, ask yourself this during the design process: What am I doing to switch my approach every few minutes? You need to *design* for engagement. Brandon Charpied, Executive Director of the Management & Organizational Behavior Teaching Society, has managed academic conferences all over the world. He suggests the following when coaching presenters: "Experience has shown that the optimal alternative is to prepare for the entirety of the 30-minute window. Devote 20 minutes to a presentation, and the remaining 10 [are] broken up into interaction (as simple as Q & A) inserted into the 10- and 20-minute marks." Think about simple interventions you can use to keep people engaged: a joke, a quick story, an amazing statistic, your enthusiasm, a micro-conversation, a rhetorical question, a written reflection, a quick video, a demonstration, audience polling, incredible slides with compelling images, a breakout discussion, a question in chat, and your skillful delivery...just to name a few.

In the context of presentations, there are few experiences worse than being stuck in a long and boring presentation. Time moves slowly, your mind is distracted, and the presenter seemingly has no idea how the audience is experiencing them. As we design for time, we keep the voice of Larry Oskowski, National Sales Senior Director at GOJO Industries, in mind. He told us, "I have found that people's attention spans just aren't what they are in person. My suggestion is to be concise, include clean slides and graphics, and ensure your presentation is well-timed."

When you are planning your presentation, then, think to yourself: How do I want the audience to experience time? How do I make the time that they're spending watching and listening to me more worthwhile than the time they could be spending doing other work?

Design for Interaction & Engagement

"It's the difference between speaker and facilitator. No matter what you are presenting, no matter who the participants are, you can ask questions, leverage chat, and use other facilitation tools to pull the audience in and engage with them."

—Jennifer Cowles, Leader of Leadership and Executive Programs at KeyBank

When presenting online, it's helpful to include a slide at the beginning that has an agenda/learning objectives (or you could even copy and paste it in the chat box, if you are not using slides). Likewise, it's helpful to include a slide that highlights norms for the session. Doing so will help participants understand *how* they should engage with you, the content, and how they can make the most out of the session.

In addition to an agenda and communicating norms, you will want to design *for* interaction and engagement—meaning you must actively plan for it to happen. Maggie Mills, the 2020 National Champion of the Public Forum Debate in the National Speech and Debate Association, reinforced this point nicely, even in the sphere of high school speech and debate competitions. She suggests that she and her partner are "always just trying to make sure that the judge is engaged and feels like a part of the debate rather than someone on the outside." We feel the same about presentations. Do people feel like they are a part of the storyline? Or are they on the outside? The following is a list of interventions that can help you provide a learning experience that does not feel like it's dragging on for participants. Include a handful of these interaction tactics in your presentation to help meet your learning objectives. Intentionally adding some of these tactics throughout your presentation will ensure that attendees will remain focused on *you*—not their email inboxes, their messages, or the clock.

> *"Make sure you have finished speaking before your audience has finished listening."*
> —Dorothy Sarnoff, actress

Interactive moments should not simply be inserted "just to be sure everyone is engaged" or at gratuitous moments to make the audience feel involved. Rather, interactive experiences should *connect to* and *enhance* the overall purpose and objectives of the presentation. We often consider three variables when choosing an interactive tool: timing, purpose, and modality.

1. *Timing* – Remember the 10-minute anecdote we shared earlier? Interactive moments can be strategically placed throughout the presentation to consistently recapture the attention of the audience.
2. *Purpose* – Does the interaction underscore a point or aid in the learning process? Will it allow you to gain some information about the audience? Or does it simply represent a "Hey, are you paying attention to me" moment? We mention the importance of pedagogical purpose here because we have been involved in too many sessions where a gratuitous poll did little to add value. For example, Maria recently attended a session that featured "test your knowledge" poll questions inserted within the Google Slides. Her observation was that this tactic "made us feel like we were in school and the teacher just wanted to be sure we were listening."
3. *Modality* – We work to incorporate various types of interactive interventions to avoid predictable patterns and learner fatigue— three slides and a poll, three slides and a poll, three slides and a poll. While some presenters may feel constrained by the online environment, there are a number of options available. The point here is that your objective would determine the best type of interaction to select, especially online.

The Chat Function – Throughout a presentation, the chat function can be used to ask/answer questions in real-time (or to collect them for a Q & A portion after the presentation), secure real-time feedback from participants, provide additional information or links, report out on small group discussions, or even serve as a tool to quickly get to know the audience (i.e., asking everyone to answer questions like "Where is everyone from?" or "What was everyone's first concert?"). It can also be used to facilitate dialogue—and admittedly, it takes some practice and skill to present *and* facilitate a dialogue, especially online when the dialogue could be happening in the chat box while you are speaking. Jennifer Cowles, Leader of Leadership and Executive Programs at KeyBank, emphasized the difficulty that she has noticed speakers have with managing these two, and also reinforced the importance of facilitation when she told us, "Right now that's the gap I'm seeing is people can present or speak, but they can't facilitate a dialogue." In other words, it is crucial for you to work toward learning how to effectively speak *and* facilitate (even if you designate a co-pilot to help you, which we will address later). We've even used the chat function as a tool to conclude the session: "Please post one word in the chat to summarize your experience today."

Tweeting or Social Media Posts – Some participants enjoy live-tweeting or posting to social media in real-time. For some, the process keeps them engaged and active in their learning. Likewise, this technique can help learners synthesize, summarize, and highlight content that resonates with them. If you are willing to offer that option, be sure to ask the host or organization in advance about social media protocol; they may expect that your presentation remains within the company. If they do permit or encourage social media interaction, address that at the beginning of the session, perhaps creating a hashtag for the session and sharing your social media username.

Polls – Polls represent a nice way to take the "pulse" of an audience, get quick responses, or gauge an audience's familiarity with or knowledge of a topic. A well-designed poll question can fuel discussion and dialogue for long periods of time. For example, during a webinar about effective learning methods for online courses that Maria attended, the presenter incorporated a poll shortly after the introduction and asked attendees to select which learning model their universities were planning to implement in the upcoming academic year. Participants were given about 1 minute to respond, and then the presenter verbally summarized the results and spoke about their significance before moving into the next part of the presentation. This poll had dual benefits: It allowed the presenter to get a sense of how many people were familiar with or would be working with certain instructional models, and it also helped attendees see how many universities were following similar models (or how many people had no idea which model to follow yet). While polls like this one can be effective moments for quickly checking in, the problem is that oftentimes, presenters do not design powerful polls and quickly move on after reporting the results. In other words, they simply ask a question for no apparent reason beyond "getting the audience involved." Ideally, polls advance the learning and help the presenter achieve their learning objectives.

"Raise Hand" – The "raise hand" function can be used for yes/no questions (or to allow attendees to indicate that they have a question or would like to speak, which we will discuss later). In essence, the presenter asks a quick and simple question like "How many are familiar with this model?" Answers to these quick questions can help presenters adjust in real-time and either spend more time explaining a concept or adding background information or moving on after being reassured that everyone knows what the presenter is referring to. In addition to quick responses, "raise hand" is also an opportunity to use the wisdom of the group. For instance, "Peter, I noticed you raised your hand. Would you be willing to share how the model has changed your work?" *Note that in the introductory remarks at the beginning of your presentation, you may want to indicate how the "raise hand" function will be used, and to confirm that you are using it.*

Breakout Rooms/Small Group Dialogue – Small group dialogue provides participants with an opportunity to reflect on the content with others. Similar to polls, we often experience presenters offering "throwaway" questions, and the breakout is more of a way to switch up the energy versus an activity that advances a learning objective. In addition, there are some important objectives for the breakout sessions that must be considered. The "question" or task you would like the participants to explore needs to be extremely clear; many participants will forget what you asked them to focus on—and will be lost when they are virtually relocated to another room. One option to help participants stay on task is to ask them to take a picture of your screen or write down the question(s) under consideration. Another consideration is time. Timing breakouts in an online presentation differs from a live presentation, so discuss the length with your contact. In our experience, it's better to provide too little time rather than too much time in the breakout. *Similar to our note about the chat function, we recommend that you include any plans for breakout rooms, discussion, and dialogue into the agenda that you share with participants so they are aware that their engagement will be requested/required at some point.*

Cartoons/Artwork – Scott has a colleague—Ed O'Malley, CEO of the Kansas Leadership Center—who quite effectively uses cartoons as an interactive activity. The cartoon highlighted below in Image 1 was drawn by Pat Byrne and is used when Ed and his team talk about the leadership concept of "Acting Experimentally." Cartoons are similar to memes in that they communicate a point of view in a quick, often visually appealing manner. As the presenter, you could share a cartoon and then use the chat, a poll, or a breakout to debrief the content. The presenter could also call on a participant to share their viewpoint.

Image 1
Acting Experimentally

Calling on Participants – Open-ended questions that are too vague will result in silence and awkward stares at the screen. "Does anyone have a contribution they would like to share?" or "What are your thoughts on this?" are questions that will often yield little response. "Janelle, would you be willing to share your thoughts on the cartoon? How about you, Joan?" will more likely yield discussion and dialogue. Calling on participants is an important part of the presenter's options for interaction, particularly if you are familiar with the people with whom you are meeting. Some presenters systematically "go around the room," while others tap people who have not yet contributed. If you do not know the people to whom you are presenting, your "co-pilot," or the host of the event, could help you elicit responses by calling on attendees. *Before your planning meetings with the person or organization who hired you, specify some of the ways you would want your audience to participate. You'll want to ask if it would be ok to call on people, or if you would request that the host/co-pilot assists you with that.*

You'll want to remember if you choose to call on people that—as we discussed earlier—you cannot control what others are doing on their devices. If a participant is doing something other than focusing on your presentation and does not have an answer to your question or asks you to repeat it, you need to be ready to respond effectively without embarrassing the person.

Shared Google Doc – A nice complement to a breakout room is a shared document where participants have an opportunity to perform a group task, record their group's answers to guided questions, or brainstorm their solutions to a problem. A shared document keeps participants on track, makes their time in breakout rooms active, and can serve as a nice takeaway for participants and the presenter. If this is the method you're going to use, have the Google Doc ready and open in a new window, and then copy and paste the link into the chat box so participants can seamlessly transition to the new task.

Reading/Handout – A reading or handout can be an effective tool, particularly if you want your attendees to be prepared with background knowledge and ready to jump into a discussion or to share their questions and comments right away. In education pedagogy, we call this the "flipped classroom" approach. The handout/slide deck can be provided to participants well ahead of the event or in real-time. If you are including a reading in your session, it's critical to be intentional about how you plan to use it. For example, a 3-minute pause for participants to read a handout with a captive audience may be a nice break from the lecture. Or, your handout could include a section for attendees to take their own notes (either digitally or printed out, if someone prefers handwriting notes). However, be careful—some participants may be on their phone, in their car, on the subway, or in other locations where they do not have access or unable to read the material quickly and easily. Keep accessibility in mind, too (which is why sharing material in advance may be preferred); individuals with visual impairment may need time to enlarge materials on their screens or may use screen readers to have the text read aloud to them, so planned "on demand" reading activities may not align with their reading abilities. On the topic of sharing materials ahead of time, Karen Gilliam, Agency Chief Learning Officer & OD Capability Lead at NASA, shared her preference for that as a way to increase her engagement. She told us, "It's really nice when I can download the slides and follow along that way." We agree; some people also learn better when they take their own notes on paper (like Maria, who took notes during all of our interviews for this project, even though the sessions were recorded on Zoom). In fact, Eileen Sheil, Vice President of Communications at Medtronic, essentially made the same comment: "I like to see the slides ahead of time, and then walk me through the deck. If I'm seeing slides for the first time in the meeting, it's more difficult to digest it all and ask a good question." These notions, for some learners, may align with your plans to "Design for Stickiness"—if they have handouts in advance and can print them out to write on them, they may be more engaged and remember more.

Activity – An activity or puzzle is an engaging way to introduce a topic or reinforce a point. An "activity" may take up 2 minutes, or 2 hours, depending on presenter objectives. An example of a quick activity is as follows: Scott will often discuss the concept of conceptual blocks, which are "mental barriers that impede an individual's ability to define or solve a problem." After providing the definition, he will often share the following puzzle, asking the participants to identify the answer:

> *"A young boy and his father were out playing football when they were caught at the bottom of a giant pileup. Both were injured*

and rushed to the hospital. They were wheeled into separate operating rooms and two doctors prepped up to work on them, one doctor for each patient. The doctor operating on the father got started right away, but the doctor assigned to the young boy stared at him in surprise. 'I can't operate on him!' the doctor exclaimed to the staff. 'That child is my son!'"

Scott then asks participants to digitally raise their hands when they have the answer(s). The story reinforces the concept. In this instance, many people have subconscious rules in their heads that surgeons are "men."

Admittedly, conducting activities in an online environment is an interesting challenge and we would love to hear your thoughts and ideas. There are a few options, though. These fun little activities catch people's attention and set a tone of curiosity and wonder.

1. If participants have a common set of supplies, perhaps the presenter tasks them with a universal challenge that requires them to build, draw, or create something.
2. There are several online resources, such as www.mural.co, that allow for visual collaboration. Resources such as Mural allow users to actively participate in ways similar to face-to-face meetings.
3. Task participants with securing a "special object" that represents their passion for the topic being discussed, their family, a hobby, or a concept.
4. Perform a quick demonstration, or some other physical manifestation of your opening point. For instance, Scott has used the **Changing Perspective Activity**[8] to discuss the importance of perspective. He has also used the **Point North Activity**[9] to highlight the challenge of getting everyone on the same page (Links to these resources can be found at www.captovation.ai/book).

Video – Similar to face-to-face presentations, video is an important tool that can emphasize a point and aid in participant learning. In an online environment, we have found that it's best to provide participants with a link in the chat and allow them to watch the video on their own equipment. Streaming a video live on your device for everyone to view through your shared screen is not recommended because you do not have control over the internet connections of participants; so while the video may play clearly on your computer and on the devices of some, others may see a choppy video where the sound skips and the picture freezes. When introducing the video, presenters should ask their host or a participant to provide a "thumbs up" or indicator when the video is complete.

For accessibility purposes, try to obtain or add in captions for any videos that you include in your presentation (and if someone is watching the video on a device where the sound does not work or in an environment where the volume needs to be low, that will be beneficial as well).

Another consideration is an audio clip from a famous speech or interview. The *History Channel* has a wonderful database to choose from. Practice this ahead of time to ensure participants can hear your audio, but this is another way to share information in a unique and different way.

Compelling Images/Graphics – Similar to cartoons, slides that feature striking images are another important feature that can aid in participant interaction and engagement. For instance, the website *Information is Beautiful* provides guests with powerful graphical images of information that can fuel dialogue, or emphasize a key point. There are also interactive websites that allow presenters to share their screen and interact with the data. For example, www.gapminder.org provides a powerful graphical representation of how an increase in income has positively impacted life expectancy.

It bears mentioning again here that you need to be mindful of the variety of devices attendees tune in on; thus, if you are incorporating images and graphics, try to keep them simple and uncluttered. One point that Micki Byrnes, Ed Markey, Eileen Sheil, and Larry Oskowski all agreed on was that slides should not be packed with complicated graphics and text. Select or create images and graphics that make it easy for the conversation to move forward, instead of spending time reading what is on the graphic or explaining everything on the image.

Thought-Provoking Question – A well-designed, well-placed, and thoughtful question can be an excellent engagement intervention. In our experience, there's a couple of important considerations. First, does the question have a little "heat" to it? In other words, is it provocative and will it spark engagement? Second, is the question open-ended and can it be explored from multiple perspectives?

Consistent Breaks – For meetings longer than an hour, it's critical to build in 5–10-minute breaks so participants can refresh and re-center. Even a quick 5-minute break can help prevent fade and ensure that participants are getting the most of your presentation or workshop. When you signal a break, remind attendees to keep themselves muted and encourage them to turn off their video momentarily, if it is not off already. When they re-enable their video, you will get a sense of when most people have returned and are ready to resume the presentation. At the beginning of the break, you could start a timer and share your screen so you can then take a quick break as well, and so you and the attendees all stay on track with a fixed amount of time.

Design for a Smooth "Day of" Experience

Displaying Expertise Across Platforms

Sharing tips and tricks for each platform is outside the scope of this book. However, whether you are using Microsoft Teams, Google Meet, Zoom, GoToMeeting, or other platforms, it's critical that you display competence. This means that if you are unfamiliar with a new platform, be sure to schedule a time to practice and clearly understand its nuances.

Negotiating the platform is a new reality, so that is why we recommend that you ask which platform you'll be using during your planning meeting; getting that information early on will give you time to read up, practice, and plan for nuances. "I am not familiar with _____ platform" is not what we want to hear from a presenter. Watch some tutorials on YouTube, read a couple of articles, and most importantly, practice. When you download and create an account for a new platform, there will often be "help" sections or tips that appear as well.

Designate a Co-Pilot

As we briefly mentioned earlier, it can be helpful to have a co-pilot for your presentation. Among other duties, this person monitors the chat function, watches for raised hands (e.g., questions), posts links, conducts the polls, keeps track of time, monitors for engagement, and places people into breakout rooms. The inclusion of the co-pilot, and how useful it can be, was underscored by Larry Oskowski, National Sales Senior Director at GOJO Industries, who told us, "We've assigned somebody in certain cases to watch for the questions as they're coming up." The co-pilot can also let the presenter know when slight hiccups have occurred (e.g., people cannot see your screen). Designating the role of co-pilot allows you to focus on *delivering* the presentation.

It's critical to determine *how* you and your co-pilot will communicate during the presentation. Will they simply interrupt and provide you with an update? Will they text you? Private message you? Scott prefers texting because it allows him to quickly glance rather than click on the chat feature while speaking.

One word of warning: The concept of the co-pilot can also diminish your impact if overused. Scott recently received an unsolicited email from Ty McTigue, Director of Enterprise Solution Sales at Acuity Brands, who commented, "The amount of times I cringe when someone on a Teams/Zoom/Skype meeting says 'next slide please' is astronomical! They lose me right at that moment...it's infuriating almost. Ask for control before you present." While we certainly acknowledge that everyone is going to have a different opinion about norms and preferences, we include all of these to emphasize the importance of making these choices consciously; if you can have control of your slides, we advocate for that, and suggest that your co-pilot help with chat and Q & A. In some instances (e.g., with multiple presenters), you may not have control of your slides.

Provide a Technology Tour

If participants are unfamiliar with the technology, the host should provide a brief tour of the technology so participants understand the basic functionalities of the software. The host should share the basics and let participants know what they should do if they have technological difficulties.

Announcements

Similar to live performances, the host should share "housekeeping" announcements regarding agenda, norms, timing, and tech support.

Outline Desired Norms

The host should ensure participants understand the norms of behavior for the session. Common norms for the host to cover include:

- *Questions* – "Please post questions in the chat function and we will address them at the end," or "Feel free to ask questions throughout. Please use the 'raise hand' function and the speaker will address your question," or "The chat box will be enabled, although I will not be able to address anything submitted until the end."
- *Audio* – "Please ensure that your audio is on mute."
- *Cameras* – "Please be sure to turn on your screens" or "Please be sure to turn on your video while in the breakout rooms."
- *Chat Function* – "Feel free to make comments, share resources, or post your feedback in the chat function throughout the session. I will periodically pause the speaker and share what I'm seeing."

Conclusion—It's All About Them

Too many presenters slap together a deck with little concern for what they are putting into motion. When Scott coaches executives, physicians, and students, he finds that it is clear when a client has designed without the audience in mind. Some indicators include: long periods of talking, low levels of interaction, a complex and cumbersome slide deck, and lack of structure (e.g., no introduction, no roadmap, and little awareness of the ultimate objective).

Another indicator is a lack of planning for the "day of" experience. When asked even the most basic questions (e.g., "what platform will you be presenting on?"), they don't have an answer. And the concepts of a practice session and a co-pilot are not even on their radar. Often, these considerations are easy enough to fix, and in the end, they will set up the presenter for success.

Our primary goal with this chapter is to prompt you to adopt the "you view" (which is a prominent viewpoint in Maria's business communications courses). Instead of viewing your presentations as an opportunity for you to be on the virtual stage and talk about what *you* know, we encourage you to think of your presentations as a chance for the *audience* to learn something important not only from you, but also from themselves as individual participants and perhaps even as a larger group. In short, this chapter reminds you to think about what it would look like to be an audience member before you even begin writing any notes or designing any slides.

In Chapter 2, we explore the concept of structure. Is your introduction captivating? Are your purpose and objective clear? Do you have a clear roadmap that is easy to follow? Is the body of your presentation tight, and does it support your overall objective? Finally, are you finishing strong and scenario-planning for the Q & A? If so, you are well on your way to excellence.

CHAPTER 2:
DESIGN YOUR STRUCTURE

"He is an effective speaker, because he is earnest, strong, honest, simple in style, and clear as crystal in his logic."

—*Hartford Evening Press,* 1860,
in reference to Abraham Lincoln

Take a moment to think about a meeting that you've attended (whether in-person or virtual) where the meeting leader either dives right into the content ("So let's take a look at last week's sales figures...") or fumbles around with how to signal that the meeting is beginning ("Um, well, it's 1:00 and I think everyone's here...so, what do we want to discuss today about customer satisfaction?"). In the first example, we imagine that you probably felt jolted into action, perhaps not quite prepared to talk about those sales figures right away. And in that second scenario, we're sure it just felt...awkward. Neither situation gives the impression that the meeting leader had a plan for the structure of the meeting beyond either the topic or the purpose. This would be similar to a presentation scenario where the speaker would just talk aimlessly; even if that speaker is the most knowledgeable person in the world about the topic, a presentation without an intentionally-designed structure is going to leave listeners confused, overwhelmed, or not knowing what they're supposed to do.

In this chapter, we discuss the importance not only of having a structure in your presentation, but also designing that structure intentionally. We examine the distinct elements that listeners expect to hear and see during their time with you, and offer suggestions for a variety of ways that each of those pieces can be built into your presentation. By planning an introduction that will hook your audience's attention and ease them into your presentation, presenting them with a clear roadmap for what your time together will include, circling back to key topics throughout the presentation, ending with something significant, and intentionally setting aside time for discussion or Q & A, you will demonstrate how highly you value an opportunity to present or lead a session.

The Introduction

As previously mentioned, most audiences have made judgments about you before you've even opened your mouth. This is one reason why your introduction is so critical. The introduction sets the tone, and if you place yourself in the role of an audience member, you know what it's like to observe a speaker who masterfully sets the appropriate tone for the occasion. Perhaps it's an intriguing tone, a somber tone, a playful tone, or a tone that communicates opportunity. For instance, Karen Gilliam, Agency Chief Learning Officer & OD Capability Lead at NASA, described the following about how she opened a meeting where the topic for the day involved issues of race: "We shared a couple of stories, quick stories, personal stories, true stories, because that opened up the space for people to say, 'Ah, you know, wow, look at what they just shared. So maybe this might be a safe space for me to engage.'" Ultimately, there are several ways to set the tone and captivate your audience from the beginning—a story, interesting facts or statistics, a provocative statement, humor, a quote, a physical activity, or even a video to grab the audience's attention. Sometimes, it's a combination of these.

Story – A well-told story is worth its weight in gold. We heard this from a few executives. Eileen Sheil, Vice President of Communications at Medtronic, asserted that "powerful stories are still really important when you're trying to connect online." And as Jennifer Cowles, Leader of Leadership and Executive Programs at KeyBank, suggests, it's important to have a "story arc that people can follow. A storyline that grabs listeners at the beginning and keeps them engaged throughout." In fact, research suggests that stories are potent interventions if we want audience members to remember our talk. The story could be intensely personal, or it could be a tale of some heroic individual or experience. The story could communicate disaster, or it could be a story of hope. Regardless, it's a story, and your choice helps draw in listeners and elicit some emotion; recall the question, "What do you want them to know, feel, and do?" You must practice your story because delivery will be critical—perhaps most important will be your vocal variety, nonverbals, and movement, if possible. It's also essential to practice because you must ensure that you have the correct timing—especially online.

Interesting Facts – In his well-received TED Talk, *Is the world getting better or worse? A look at the numbers*,[10] Stephen Pinker provides a litany of statistics designed to attack common assumptions that we hold as human beings (he also uses strong images and a quote). In his case, it's the narrative that "everything is going to hell!"[11] Pinker beautifully presents data that flies in the face of this master narrative. If your talk is about longevity and lifespan, perhaps some statistics about contemporary studies will grab your audience's attention.

Alternatively, if you are building a case for parents vaccinating their children, maybe you provide some NIH data that will surprise or engage listeners.

A Provocative Statement – A provocative statement is a surefire way to secure the attention of your audience—especially if you are with an audience that does not expect it. In his book *Lifespan*, Harvard geneticist David Sinclair writes the following statement: "Aging research today is at a similar stage as cancer research was in the 1960s. … From the looks of it aging is not going to be that hard to treat—far easier than curing cancer."[12] Statements like this will need to be backed up with facts, data, and logic, and in the book, he does just that. You must build a logical case for your assertion, but this is one surefire way to get people engaged and interested in what you have to say.

Humor – In some instances, it is not appropriate to include humor. In other instances, you may not feel comfortable adding in humor, which is perfectly fine. However, it is an option, and *can* set the tone and capture the attention of your audience, which is why many presenters begin their talk with a story, anecdote or lighthearted joke. If nothing else, it's a way to connect with the audience and let them get to know *you* in a small way; or as Mary Hirsch says, "Humor is a rubber sword—it allows you to make a point without drawing blood." A particular type of humor is self-deprecating humor, which is another way to connect and let the audience know that you do not take yourself too seriously. Use that carefully and sparingly if you do, though, because you do not want to undercut your credibility with constant self-criticism.

A Quote – A well-constructed quote can set the tone for your entire presentation. For instance, Scott often begins a discussion on presentation skills with the following quote by Steve Jobs: "People who know what they are talking about don't need PowerPoint." In addition to being a good quote, it's also a bit provocative and always yields some lively debate from members of the audience. A side note about quotes; do your best to ensure to attribute the quote to the correct individual, since there is a lot of misinformation on the internet. Likewise, ensure that you consider your audience when beginning with a quote.

While a quote can be great in spirit, if it is *too* controversial or provokes too much discussion, you could lose the true focus of your presentation.

A Video – When discussing the concept of personal change, Scott recently saw a speaker begin with the video *The Backwards Brain Bicycle*[13], and everyone was captivated from the beginning. He was using the video to be provocative, but it also added some humor and mesmerized the audience from the very beginning. Scott also attended a presentation on empathy that began with the video *Empathy: The Human Connection to Patient Care*[14] from Cleveland Clinic (Links to these videos can be found at www.captovation.ai/book). Now, starting with a video can be a little tricky, but it's one fundamental approach to capturing the attention of your audience.

The Purpose/Objective

> *"Is there a purpose to it so you know why you're there from the start? Is it clear? And at the beginning, [there should be] a roadmap of 'here's how it's going to go' so you know what to expect."*
>
> —Ed Markey, Vice President of Corporate Communications at Goodyear Tire & Rubber Co.

At times, it's entirely appropriate to let the audience know the conclusion you have reached at the beginning. Your audience, the situation, and how you expect them to react will help you determine whether you design your presentation following the direct strategy, or the indirect strategy.

If you follow the direct strategy and open your presentation by stating your conclusion, you build the case in the body of your presentation. When following the direct strategy, you would want to state your objective at the end of your introduction, and right before you present the roadmap. Be sure that you use clear language that signals that you are stating your objective—choose a tone that aligns with your purpose, whether that is to inform or persuade. Sample thesis statements may include:

- Based on our cost analysis and benchmarking, we should move forward with Project XYZ.
- In the final analysis, Steve Jobs was more of a visionary than a leader of people.
- We are well on our way to increasing human lifespan and healthspan by upwards of 30 years.
- There has never been a better time to live on Planet Earth than today.
- The world is more democratic today than any other time in world history.

Essentially, you begin with the punchline and then build your case, so others see what you see. This may only work for certain audiences and situations, though—those where you believe your audience will be receptive to your message, or if you are making a decision for your company or organization and communicating it to your employees. In other situations, you will want to follow the indirect strategy of organization, where your objective statement is presented later in the presentation. If you believe that your audience may respond either neutrally or negatively to your message, then it might be more effective to spend the body of your presentation presenting facts, data, and other evidence to support your main point. Using the material discussed in the beginning of Chapter 1 as you think about your audience will help you determine where your objective will be presented most effectively.

The Roadmap

A roadmap helps listeners follow your overall trajectory, and is equally important to share with the audience in presentations given in-person and online. Scott Taylor, Owner & Creative Director at BlkDog, described his roadmap this way when reflecting on one of his own presentations: "My presentation consisted of five main points, and I made sure to list them all at the onset, calling each one out to the audience as an oral signpost of where we were headed. Within each main point, I added two bullet points to serve as reminders and visual cues for the audience to understand my research and provide context."

You would be amazed at how often speakers fail to do what Scott Taylor suggests—set forth a clear layout of how their presentation will go for their audience. As a result, the message becomes lost, muddled, or unclear. An outline of the presentation's content sets your audience at ease, helps them follow along, and reinforces key points. Speakers who consistently revisit their roadmap by including oral signposts (which are also discussed in Chapter 5), or include signals on their slides like numbers, Roman numerals, and/or the same subject titles presented in the roadmap shown at the beginning, ensure a clear and concise message. At times, people think that a roadmap equals a rigid and formulaic delivery, requiring consistent signposts like "Now, we will move to agenda item 5." This is not the case. Excellent presenters will weave in and out of their roadmap in a conversational tone. They reinforce critical content, and perhaps most importantly, keep themselves on track. So once a speaker has concluded their introduction and objective statement (if applicable), the following statement would help listeners know what's to come:

> I have shared some incredible statistics with you and suggested that we can increase human lifespan by upwards of 30 years within the next couple of decades. Moving forward, I will share how, and our research suggests three primary methods: 1) preventative medicine, 2) regenerative medicine, and 3) diet and intermittent fasting. I will conclude with a quick summary and a fascinating statistic. First, preventative medicine...
>
> *Further along in the presentation...*"so preventative medicine is our first method for increasing lifespan. Our second is regenerative medicine..."
>
> *A little later...*"so preventative medicine is our first method for increasing lifespan. Regenerative medicine is our second method. The third method is diet and intermittent fasting."
>
> *And toward the end (review and conclusion)...*"today, we have discussed three approaches that based on our research, are critical to increasing lifespan: preventative medicine, regenerative medicine, and diet/intermittent fasting. These three approaches will increase our lifespan by upwards of 30 years. According to a 2009 ABC News story, *Most Babies Born Today May Live Past 100*, more than half of babies born today will live

to be more than 100. That means a baby born today has more than a 50% chance to see 2120! Now think back to 1920—100 years *ago*. Can you even imagine the world they will see? I am excited to hear your thoughts and would welcome questions or comments..."[15]

As a listener, you can see how easy it is to follow along. If the speaker's objective is for the audience to remember the three approaches, repetition is required and appreciated by the audience. It's incumbent on the presenter to continually revisit and repeat key points. It can feel like overkill for the speaker, but for the listener, it's appreciated and aids in retention. Be sure that you rely on either the same terms or similar language when you are incorporating the oral signpost reminders (as you can see in the examples above) to make it clear to your audience that you are moving forward through the agenda.

The Body

The body of the presentation is the centerpiece of your talk; you might think that this section needs the most time and attention in terms of design, but the introduction and conclusion sometimes might need just as much, or even more! By the time you reach this point, your introduction, objective, and roadmap have set the stage, and the body is designed to build your case or reinforce that objective. Barbara Minto's Pyramid Principle (sometimes called McKinsey's Pyramid Principle[16]) offers a useful heuristic for designing the body of your argument.[17] Using the example of longevity from the previous section, Minto would challenge the speaker to develop three supporting points for each of the three main approaches: 1) preventative medicine, 2) regenerative medicine, and 3) diet and intermittent fasting. These could be research results, statistics, or other supporting documentation. For example, the structure could look like this:

Method #1: Preventative Medicine
- Supporting research/statement 1—cost reduction
- Supporting research/statement 2—early detection
- Supporting research/statement 3—increase in productivity

Method #2: Regenerative Medicine
- Supporting research/statement 1—repairs tissue/organs
- Supporting research/statement 2—reduces pain
- Supporting research/statement 3—reduced risk of future injury

Method #3: Diet/Intermittent Fasting
- Supporting research/statement 1—reduces inflammation
- Supporting research/statement 2—lowers blood pressure, cholesterol
- Supporting research/statement 3—burns ketones vs. carbohydrates

The main objective of the body of your presentation is to support the overall thesis or objective of the discussion (i.e., *we are on the path to extending human lifespan by upwards of 30 years*). The material you include in the middle of your presentation builds the case and convinces the audience that you have done your research and are speaking from a position of expertise. While we have only provided headers (e.g., cost reduction or restores function) for each supporting research/statement, it's easy to see how you would begin to build in research, data, and supporting evidence for each. By doing so, you are further building your case.

Above all, this supporting content must be relevant, accurate, and balanced. In other words, you are providing the full picture, even if some aspects are inconclusive or still in process. For instance, the assumption is that growing organs with your own cells is possible, but it's not there yet, and likely will not be for years to come. In addition, we suggest you use the Assertion-Evidence (AE) approach to slide design discussed in Chapter 3. This approach combines strong visuals (e.g., graphs, images) with factual statements to communicate your message.

Whatever you choose for the body of your presentation ultimately reflects back onto you and your credibility. That means you must choose both your words and the words of others who you are quoting wisely. If you are pulling in outside research, ensure that the sources are reliable; if you are incorporating company or industry data, be sure that the numbers are correct and are as recent as possible. And as you reach the end of a "main point" or "main section," incorporate the verbal version of what Maria calls a *point sentence* when she teaches writing; this point sentence represents a direct tie back to your main objective or purpose statement, and answers the crucial "so what?" question. You don't want your audience thinking "what did that anecdote/data/visual have to do with this topic?", so do the work *for* them by drawing an imaginary line between the body material and your purpose with that point sentence (if you prefer to write notes out in advance, you can test this by seeing if you can indeed draw a line between the section notes and something in your objective statement).

Once you have made it through the body of the session, take a deep breath—you got through one of the most stressful parts! You've probably just presented your audience with a lot of information, so a good strategy is to take a step back to review. For many, it will be their first time hearing your talk, so as we mentioned, using the rhetorical technique of repetition is an effective choice.

Review Your Roadmap

In the review section, summarize what you have said. Summarize the objective (or, if you are following the indirect strategy, present the objective in its straightforward and strongest form) and the main points. There is a sample review/conclusion in the roadmap section of this chapter. For the veterans of this topic, this is the "tell them what you told them" segment of the talk. For example:

> I mentioned at the beginning of the presentation that we need to invest in artificial intelligence. It's clear that our competitors are aggressively investing in machine learning; there is clear cost-saving after an initial investment, and this approach allows us to monetize the data we will collect.

The Path Forward/Recommendations

At times, you may be charged with providing a path forward. In other words, you will be asked to answer the question, "now what?" If this is the case, it's essential to return to the Minto Method as you build the case for your path forward. Be sure to gain clarity on the requests in your specific context, but a clear statement with a few logical supporting statements will likely suffice. An example would be as follows:

I mentioned at the beginning of the presentation that we need to invest in artificial intelligence. It's clear that our competitors are aggressively investing in machine learning; there is clear cost-saving after an initial investment, and this approach allows us to monetize the data we will collect. Moving forward, I am recommending that we make an initial capital expenditure of three million dollars so we can pilot the technology in the additives division. The additives division has the team in place, is our most "at-risk" division, and its leader, Hanna Johnson, has led similar turnarounds with great success. It's a win all around.

The Conclusion

Your conclusion is the audience's final opportunity to hear from you. In many ways, it's just as important as the introduction. End using the same techniques listed in the introduction section: a quote, a story, or an inspirational video can each be a way to conclude. Other good options for a meaningful conclusion include:

Return to Mission – If the organization has a mission/vision statement or principles that publicly communicate its aspirations, use their words to conclude. For instance, if you've presented an innovative solution and "always innovates" is a value held by the organization, it's a great way to align your idea or perspective with the organization's aspirations.

A Better Future – Paint a picture for the audience. Help participants see how your solution will impact them and their work. Help them understand how your intervention will lead to a better future: one that is free from some of their current challenges and roadblocks.

The Bookend – Return to your introduction to help the audience see how the situation or story could have turned out differently, how your idea would have helped, or how your solution will yield a better future. Perhaps your bookend also charts a new path that will help the organization meet its mission.

Call to Action – Provide listeners with a "next step," way to engage, or plea for action. For instance, at the conclusion of a presentation on sustainability, call on listeners to recycle and begin a composting program at home. The call to action is a great way to encourage action, participation, and the opportunity to make a difference.

Quote – Conclude with a powerful quote that synthesizes your main point or key takeaway. A powerful quote from a well-respected person in your domain can align your presentation with seminal thinkers who align with your perspective.

Story/Anecdote – Concluding with a well-told story is a powerful way to solidify your main point in the minds of listeners. Be sure the story is well-structured, delivered with mastery, and aligns with your primary objective. Doing so will leave your audience with a strong and lasting impression of you.

Rhetorical Question – Challenging the audience to think critically about their own perspectives, opinions, or assumptions can be a powerful way to move people beyond their current way of being. Likewise, rhetorical questions cause listeners to reflect on their behaviors, actions, or lack of action.

Summarize Your Main Points – Tell them what you told them. Doing so at the very end is your final opportunity to ensure that listeners walk away from your presentation with a strong command of your main points.

Signal the End With Instructions – Rhetorically signal the end of the presentation portion and indicate that Q & A will begin or that you will look at any questions raised in the chat box. If you have a co-pilot, you can call on that person to summarize or start asking you some of the questions: "Sarah, I know you have been monitoring the chat during this presentation. Are there any specific topics or questions that have come up for me to address?"

The Q & A

Question and answer sessions (those at the end of a presentation where the audience can ask questions) can be stressful. They take away your control as a presenter, since you have no idea what questions are coming and how you will answer them. Some level of anxiety is completely normal (and probably good). If you expect perfection, you are going to have a difficult time. It will not be perfect. In the heat of the moment, there are some concrete measures you can take to navigate the Q & A more effectively.

First, remember that you are still "on" and it will be essential to focus on your timing. From a timing perspective, you do not want to jump in too quickly, or cut off the person with the question. Online presentations can make this aspect of timing even more complicated, since internet speeds vary and participants are not always in the same room to see who wants to speak next. Our suggestion is to be patient while a person asks a question and wait to respond until after you are 100% sure their question is finished (an extra second of silence will also help you collect your thoughts). Remember that your delivery is still a priority. Many presenters are so relieved to be done that they forget they are "on" and slip into space fillers, a tone that is too conversational, and so forth.

This is also where you will want to remind everyone of the Q & A rules that you noted at the beginning of the presentation. If you have encouraged participants to submit questions in the chat box throughout your presentation, you can begin the Q & A by asking your co-pilot if any themes emerged (i.e., "There are a number of questions about how long it will take to ship this product batch out, so could you address that?") or to relay specific questions. You could also say, "Please use the 'Raise hand' feature if you have a question. My co-pilot will call on those who have raised their hands." *It is crucial for YOU to address these expectations—otherwise, people will talk over each other or multiple people will try to start asking a question simultaneously...which does nothing but waste time!* If you have control, you could also call on people who you assume will be well-intended to begin.

Once the question is asked, take the time to smile, repeat, and acknowledge (repeating the question will also help your audience, in case they missed what was asked). At times, presenters will let the discussion "speed up" on them. A great way to combat this is to slow down the pace of the conversation intentionally. For instance, saying, "Thank you, very insightful...so the question is about the potential downside of us making this investment. First, I think this is a critical question, and I am sure there are many perspectives in the room. For me though, a few issues deserve consideration as a starting place for dialogue…".

After you answer, you have at least a couple options:

- See if others in the room have thoughts or perspectives and simply facilitate.
- See if specific people have additional thoughts. Maybe they have content expertise that could add value.
- Move on to another question.
- If you do not know the answer, acknowledge the individual, and let the audience know you will find the answer and get back with them quickly. The key is to enter the Q & A space with humility, curiosity, and preparation.

Humility – You cannot possibly know everything. If you know you have done your best to prepare, remain open to other possibilities and perspectives that audience members may bring to the conversation. It's in that space that new ground can be covered. Scott will often say, "There are many ways to think about this topic; this is what's been top of mind for me in recent months, and I am excited to hear what you have been thinking about as well." When presented with a new perspective, Maria will respond with, "That is a great perspective, and I have not thought about it from that angle yet" before continuing. Acknowledging the question in this way gives validity to the contributor, allows Maria some time to think, and diminishes the "I don't know" aspect of the response so that attendees don't dwell on wondering, "she didn't think about that?"

Curiosity – If you are truly curious, you know that there's likely more work to do, more to learn, and additional research to be conducted. Whether it's a scientific paper, a proposed strategy for your business, or some other type of proposal, letting your ego take a back seat to the wonderment of the puzzle can be a "freeing" approach to the Q & A period. In essence, you show up as an individual who knows they do not have all the answers (humility) and a person who is genuinely interested in moving closer to the truth (curiosity). You can demonstrate this openness to continue learning to your audience by acknowledging topics you might want to explore in more detail or noting questions that you hadn't thought about before, as mentioned above. Demonstrating to your audience that you want to know what *they* want to know, and that you will continue working within the topic, will illustrate your curiosity.

Preparation – If you are prepared, you have anticipated the questions, hot buttons, and criticisms of your presentation and planned how you might respond to them. However, we were reminded by Micki Byrnes, President & General Manager at WKYC-TV, about the importance of preparation when she stated, "We see some folks on Zoom [who] are not doing a great job. It's because you know damn well, they're faking it, and they're trying to tap dance their way through stuff. And it's very easy to know." She's right. If you are presenting at your best, you have proactively addressed some of these in the body of your presentation. In addition, maybe you include extra slides *after* your final slide that you can draw upon if people have questions, comments, or concerns. Or perhaps you let the audience know that you are open to further dialogue after the formal presentation to further explore ideas. Some will try to lure you into doing so *during* the presentation; if this happens, a great approach is to say, "That's a longer conversation, but I would love to have it with you. Maybe we can connect after?" Here are some other concrete ideas that you can prioritize before you speak:

- Know your triggers, and do not get sucked in if an audience member has ill intentions or a disagreeable nature.
- Don't put pressure on yourself to be perfect.
- Know some key statistics that work in most situations.
- Plant someone in the audience who is willing to provide honest feedback on your performance.

Above all, it is vital that you *intentionally make time* for Q & A in your presentation; try to dedicate at least 10 minutes at the end for the audience to respond with their thoughts and questions, or even request clarifications or talk through next steps. This is a great time to do a "soft handoff" of control from you over to the host and/or the attendees, especially if the conversation moves toward creating an action plan that the group can take away and continue working on.

Conclusion—Map Your Route

Steve Jobs once said something that we believe is important and relevant when beginning to plan your session: "Simple can be harder than complex: You have to work hard to get your thinking clean to make it simple. But it's worth it in the end because once you get there, you can move mountains." When it comes to determining and communicating your overall purpose and identifying what you want participants to learn, feel, or do as a result of your presentation, clean thinking is critical.

Great presenters draw listeners into a conversation right away with a captivating introduction. They set the table with their roadmap, use logic and storytelling to build the case, and wrap up their talk by leaving the audience with a powerful and lasting impression. To imagine it another way, think of this: a clean structure is like the foundation of a house. It forms the base for what everything else rests upon, and thus must be strong, secure, and consistently reinforced. The elements that are built on it, then, include a beautiful deck, an elegant delivery, and a great audience experience. All of these pieces require careful, intentional design.

Speaking of beautiful decks, that's what Chapter 3 is all about. The ultimate objective is for your audience to say "wow" when they look at your deck. We want your slide design to be engaging, beautiful, and *complementary* to both you and your ultimate objective. Sound complicated? Read on to learn about the best ways to (easily) create a compelling visual presentation.

CHAPTER 3:
DESIGN YOUR VISUALS

"We have met the Devil of Information Overload and his impish underlings, thecomputer virus, the busy signal, the dead link, and the PowerPoint presentation."

—James Gleick, author

Visual aids are important accompaniments to your presentation, and can serve a number of important purposes—some of which have been discussed earlier. They spark conversation and thought, illustrate important points, highlight ideas, and provide visual variety from text. However, as with the rest of your presentation, visual aids must be intentionally designed; if they're too simple or uncontextualized, audiences will be confused about their relevance. If they're too complex or unreadable, the audience's attention will be on the visual, not on you. This chapter will examine ways of carefully planning and designing your slide deck.

David Rae, President/Co-Founder of 503 Media & Events and the founder of TEDxPortland, provided us with a quick checklist of his must-haves for visuals: "crisp, designed, supportive slides in the 16:9 format." He also wants a dark background and strong images with little to no copy so participants are not squinting to see what's on your shared screen. He's also a big fan of sending the deck ahead of time to the audience so participants can view on their own terms. In addition, he says, "Don't show up with a thumbnail photograph—meaning you are hiding and are not prepared to present your virtual self."

Design Your Slide Deck

Imagine this scenario (maybe you've been in it already): The online presentation begins with the presenter displaying the first slide of a dense deck, and then they utter, "We have a lot to get through, so we better jump right in." You know right away that for the next 45 minutes, you are the reluctant participant in a "PowerPoint Death March." Sadly, you're not wrong. As the presentation continues, you are presented with slide after slide of dense material—paragraphs of text, complex graphs and charts that are hard to read, and so many shapes and explanations and arrows that the slides look like a Perfection game board. This is not an uncommon experience given Microsoft's estimates that more than 1.25 million PowerPoint presentations occur *every hour*.[18] Of course, this reality has resulted in many people who abuse this tool; in his book *The Cognitive Style of PowerPoint,* Yale professor Edwin Tufte wrote that PowerPoint is "making us stupid, degrading the quality and credibility of our communication."[19] The executives we interviewed also consistently reinforced the importance of crisp, clean, and easily understandable slides.

Scott teaches with a colleague who coaches people to think of each slide as a billboard. Billboards often feature a strong image and one central message that is quickly understood. This is such an illustrative and impactful metaphor—and while we acknowledge that this advice is not appropriate and relevant in some instances, in most cases, it's a good rule of thumb. Another way to think about your slides is as notecards that may have crisp and powerful images. While most people don't realize it, slide design is critical to your success.

In fact, we found the results of one study quite interesting. And in some respects, those study results support Rae's assertion, which is highlighted at the beginning of the chapter. The authors found that:

> Having slides with large amounts of text is one of the main signals that the visual aid is not really helping the presentation. The number of images (TNI) is the second most important feature. The impact of this feature is positive, meaning that a large number of images is correlated with better slides. Number of tables (NT) is third with a negative relation (more tables, lower grade) and the Maximum Font Size (MAXFS) is fourth with a positive relation (larger font, higher grade).[20]

All too often, we witness presenters setting themselves up for failure. They design decks that are too challenging to deliver. In some cases, creating an "ideal slide deck" is challenging; there might be too much text and too many visuals that absolutely need to be shared, or complex charts that must be included. This ends up meaning that you have to create too many slides, and there is just not enough time in which to reasonably cover everything. The result? An overwhelming and stressful presentation, both for you and for the audience. In these cases, we point to a single design flaw: most presenters are thinking about themselves, not the audience, when they design their decks.

Remedying that problem is easy and goes back to your mindset, as we discussed at the beginning of this book. As you design your deck, keep one concept in mind: user experience. Do your visuals engage? Are they attractive? Does your content connect? Does your design accentuate the most important ideas? Are people impressed by the appearance of your deck? Are *you* excited to deliver your deck? If not, it's a missed opportunity.

Ultimately, you do not want to set yourself up with a deck that is going to be difficult to deliver. Perhaps more importantly, you do not want to present a set of slides that will be too complex to remember. The following section highlights several dimensions of slide design to consider as you plan. The best practices represent our opinions and are based on years of working with people to design extraordinary presentations. We also incorporate recommendations based on presentations we have designed for classrooms, conferences, and professional environments.

Developing a Theme

The work of slide design experts Nancy Duarte and Garr Reynolds beautifully highlights the ways that they develop a coherent theme for their decks. Exploring the work of these two experts will provide context for this section. Perhaps you will choose to use striking black and white images with a bold font, or white background with sharp images that "pop." If the organization that hires you would like you to use their company logo or an in-house background, be sure you adhere to that as well. Developing a theme is accomplished in many ways—primarily through consistent use of images, fonts, and colors. At first, it can be challenging to design a theme because that may mean finding photographs that hang together or follow your message; this can take time and energy. However, the approach becomes more comfortable with experience.

Best practices include:

- trying to tie your images together in a way that does not require you to add a lot of verbal contextualization and explanation. Decks with images that jump from a space shuttle to an eagle to a lake to a chessboard can be distracting. If your images vary widely, your audience must intuitively understand why.
- avoiding stock templates. Doing so can communicate "novice" to your audience. The best slide decks have their own design, tone, and feel.
- resisting the feeling that a theme should be complex and complicated. A strong logo in the bottom right-hand corner, with skilled use of font and text placement, is one example of a simple but compelling theme.

Number of Slides

You do not need *a lot* of slides for this style of presentation; in fact, you don't want your entire presentation to be taken up by showing slides, because that won't leave any room for participation, breaks, or the Q & A. As Marc Gillinov, MD, Chair of the Department of Thoracic & Cardiovascular Surgery at Cleveland Clinic suggests, "Make the visuals more compelling and include a smaller number—it really has to be narrowed down." Remember, your slides are simply accenting you and your message. This is also where handouts or ancillary materials can be used to your advantage; if you have technical information that needs to be communicated, provide participants with a handout, insert the information in the notes, or place the technical slides after your formal presentation so you can reference them in a Q & A if needed. Most presenters put too much content on their slides because they are afraid they will forget a point, do not know the content, or want to be prepared if someone asks a tough question. Design around these genuine concerns and consider how many slides (or how few, if you want to look at it that way) are really needed for your presentation.

Slide Transitions & Text Animations

Minimize the use of transitions and animations, whether between slides or between bullet points, as much as possible. First, transitions and animations add complexity when your brain is already multitasking. Second, animations between slides (e.g., the checkerboard) should be avoided for accessibility purposes (and could cause dizziness!). Third, animations in between bullet points cause you to look away from the camera each time you add another piece of content. As a result, you are multitasking between the audience and the screen. Making all of the content on a slide visible from the beginning will allow you to deliver your material with excellence and keep your attention on the audience, as opposed to the screen and the clicker. Marc Gillinov, MD at Cleveland Clinic said, "A lot of people like to animate their PowerPoint slides. I don't think that comes over as well in virtual presentation. Just show them the entire slide—right off the bat. I think you have less time as the speaker to capture attention and you have less time overall."

Another reason to avoid using an animation for each bullet point is because, as Maria has experienced many times, you may lose track of how many bullet points you have, as well as what each one says (unless you have notes or a handout of your slides in front of you). Then you may find yourself talking ahead of the bullet points and covering material *before* it's projected—and then when you advance your slide and another point appears, you will end up saying "and as I've already mentioned…"

Constructing Your Written Content

> *"Drop the bullet points. Have you ever wondered why they are called bullet points? What do bullets do? Bullets kill! And t hey will kill your presentation."*
>
> —Melissa Marshall, educator

Composing the Text

While you may have a solid structure and an outline in your written notes (and all you want to say based on your knowledge and experience), translating that text onto a slide is a step that often requires further synthesis and refinement. Because you have a limited amount of space to work with, and because you do not want to overwhelm your audience with a lengthy slide deck, the text you do include for your slides needs to communicate your sentiment in relatively few words. The challenge that comes along with that is to retain *clarity* and *relevance*, and to remember that what is on your slides must highlight only the most important points that you want the audience to remember. It should also complement what you are planning to say, not detract your audience's attention from their focus on you.

The content you *do* choose to include must fulfill three objectives: a) flag you, the presenter, of the next topic, b) communicate a point of emphasis to your audience, and c) support your overall logic and structure (i.e., it's not noise that clutters your overall message). On this point, we are reminded of what Steve Jobs once said: "You have to work hard to get your thinking clean." All too often we experience presenters who have not taken the time to do so. They cut and paste full sentences of text from another document into a PowerPoint, and in the process, "kill" their message. It becomes bullet after bullet after bullet, which is why we love the quote at the beginning of this section. Just to be clear: bullet points are not inherently bad, it's just that they are often used incorrectly.

Amount of Text

> *"I think it goes back to too many words on a slide. It's just mind-boggling how much people try to load into their presentations. The audience tends to start reading the words rather than listening to and absorbing the content. Sometimes I will turn off my video and just listen. Then, I actually gain more of the information I need."*
>
> —Eileen Sheil, Vice President of Communications at Medtronic

There are several rules of thumb regarding the amount of text you should place on a slide. The amount depends on your culture, audience, objective, and purpose. However, if you do choose to include a lot of text, realize that it will more than likely diminish your ability to be a great presenter. We agree with Karen Gilliam, Agency Chief Learning Officer & OD Capability Lead at NASA, who told us, "The creativity and the aesthetics that go along with a nice, engaging PowerPoint becomes even more important in the virtual world because the last thing you want to do is stare at a lot of words."

Here are some other reasons to be judicious with the amount of text you place on your slides. First, at least one study found that "the number of slides used in college lectures did not affect teaching effectiveness. However, slides containing no more than three bullet points and 20 or fewer words were more effective than slides with higher density."[21] Second, including a lot of text will draw you to the screen or monitor, which means that the vast majority of your time will be spent looking down or away and *not* at your audience. Third, you will be competing with the text. If you have multiple sentences or even a full paragraph on the screen, your audience will spend their time reading the words on the slide instead of watching and listening to you. In other words, you will be competing with your deck for the attention of the audience. As a result, we encourage speakers to cut down on as much text as possible. Failing to do so will more than likely stifle their ability to succeed *before they have even begun*.

Best practices include:

- If you have a lot of content you would like to convey, create a handout that accompanies your presentation and is shared in advance of the session. You could also add ancillary information in the "Notes" section of your slides so attendees can refer back later.
- Think of your slide as a notecard or a visual prompt, including just enough to speak from and keep you on track.
- As Scott would say, "Kill the text." Be ruthless about the content you choose to keep in your final version of the deck.
- Ensure that every word is an absolute must. Some strategies for reducing text include eliminating words, combining thoughts or summarizing, reducing redundancies, and deleting content that you already know you are going to say.
- Think of each slide as a billboard; every slide should have one central message.

Text Placement

The audience expects your deck to follow the well-trodden path that many before you have traversed: headers, bullets, and a text-heavy slide (i.e., the default settings). You can stand out by placing your text in unique and different locations on the slide. However, in general, do not type text over an image—use white or free space for text. Strategies of visual design indicate that a reader's eyes follow a "Z" pattern on an image like a slide or an advertisement, so design your deck with that pattern in mind.

Best practices include:

- Avoid too much layering (e.g., image overlaying image, text on image).
- Use a consistent placement style throughout your presentation. This approach will help develop your style or theme for the deck.
- Leave enough space around and between areas of text to enhance readability and cut down on reader fatigue.

Font Selection, Color, & Size

If you explored the websites for Duarte and Reynolds that were referenced in the previous section, you would notice how both use fonts with great intentionality. The font style, color, and size are tools that can help you design for the attention of the audience, and deserve as much time and intentionality as all of the other pieces. So if you want your deck, and the content therein, to stand out and make an impression, the font is an important consideration. You can experiment with font styles, colors, sizes, and placement if you feel that is appropriate, or you can choose a more traditional combination if your presentation needs to be a bit more on the formal and understated side.

Best practices include:

- Use a consistent style throughout your presentation. This approach will help develop your style or theme for the slide deck.
- Avoid fonts that are difficult to read, and avoid black Times New Roman if you want to stand out.
- Restrain from mixing multiple fonts on your slides, especially if

your chosen fonts have contrasting personalities. For example, in a presentation about mental health where you are discussing the common characteristics of depression, you would not want to put the heading of a slide in a fun and lighthearted font while the information on the slide itself is in a more straightforward font.
- Highlight keywords in your text by putting them in bold, changing the font style or size, or adding color.

Constructing Your Visual Content

Image Selection

The Assertion-Evidence (AE) approach to slide design suggests that slides with an assertion should be accompanied by a graph or image.[22] This approach juxtaposes the Common Practice (CP) approach to slides, which in large part relies on the default settings of the software (e.g., bullet points, header/title). In one study, an audience who viewed an AE-designed presentation displayed "superior comprehension and recall of information" than an audience who viewed a CP-designed presentation.[23] To explore this topic in greater depth, visit https://www.assertion-evidence.com.

If you are choosing your own images (that is, not using images provided by the person or organization that hired you), be sure that you use high-definition images from high-quality sources. Many corporations have marketing departments with professional photos, so you could inquire about that during the presentation design phase. There are several websites that have professionally taken images that are free to adopt (e.g., www.pexels.com, www.thenounproject.com, or even working within the Microsoft Office Suite). You can conduct an image search of a topic such as "fish" with the usage rights/"labeled for reuse" filter chosen; Microsoft Office will allow you to search for images with a Creative Commons license.

When you insert an image into your slide, take note of its original size. If you find yourself enlarging an image to make it fit (stretching horizontally or vertically), or adjusting it in any way (other than decreasing the size), it's likely the image will present as pixelated; this communicates a lack of professionalism. If you need to resize the image, try to expand from a corner of the image; stretching in this way will automatically adjust the horizontal and vertical orientation of the image in a neater way.

Best practices include:

- Intuitively align the image with the content of the slide; if the image stands alone, it is your responsibility to help the viewer understand why they are looking at an eagle when you are discussing profit margins.
- Choose images that are free of "water marks" or "stamps."
- Ensure that the image is sharp and clear.
- Use only one image per slide. Multiple images on one slide can clutter, obscure your message, and overwhelm the viewer.
- Avoid the use of "cute" images (e.g., bunnies, or kittens) in corporate settings.
- Steer away from stock clip art, animated GIFs, and overused images (e.g., the creepy, white, faceless people featured in any number of teamwork or leadership images on the internet).

If you are looking for inspiration or want to learn from examples, we suggest that you review *Slide:ology: The Art and Science of Creating Great Presentations* by Nancy Duarte[24] or *Presentation Zen: Simple Ideas on Presentation Design and Delivery* by Garr Reynolds.[25] Their sample slide decks are thoughtfully designed and inspirational for viewers. It is also important to provide captions for any images that you use, as depicted in Image 2. These could be placed in smaller text under or next to the photo, or added in through an "alt tag" that is hidden, but would be read aloud if an attendee is using a screen reader to view your presentation. Captions for images ensure that you are accounting for accessibility, and are simply short descriptions of what appears in an image.

Image 2
Sample Slide With an Alt Tag for Images

In 2019, **4,477,114** acres were destroyed by fire in the United States. Over the same period in 2020, more than **8,608,646** acres had burned.

Description of image to the left. A black and white photo of a dead tree. Image from: https://www.pexels.com/photo/black-and-white-black-and-white-branches-cloudy-216695/

Source: https://www.nifc.gov/fireInfo/nfn.htm

Graphs & Charts

Overheard often during the months that followed the sudden shift to online work and learning (and even beyond that): "I know you can't read this, but…", "I know there is a lot on here, but I really just want you to focus on number five in the third column…", and "There's a lot here, but I have circled the item I want you to pay attention to…".

Graphs, charts, and visuals can make or break a presentation. More often than not, we struggle to understand the charts and visuals of presenters. As a result, their message becomes muddied, unclear, and confusing. A vague message (or one that has too many shapes, directional arrows, and explanatory text on it) is frustrating for the audience. You don't want viewers to spend all their time scrutinizing the graph or chart to try and decipher it; they will end up overwhelmed and will give up before they grasp the point. There are many questions to consider before designing a chart or visual:

- What is the central message of this chart? Is this clearly communicated?
- Would the billboard-level message suffice, or is a chart the best solution?
- Is the chart clearly labeled so the audience will quickly understand?
- Is the source referenced on the slide so participants have this information?
- Is the graph or chart visually appealing?
- Will the chart be easy to navigate for you as the presenter?

Best practices include:

- When possible, only include the billboard-level message. Then, place the full chart after your final slide. If audience members want more detail beyond your billboard-level analysis, you have the more detailed version on hand.
- Have a few people who are unfamiliar with your content view the graph or chart. Do they quickly understand your central message?
- Do not add extra text, images, or clutter to a slide with a graph or chart (e.g., pictures).
- Use the header as your punchline to emphasize your central message.

Use of Embedded Video/Animation

There are some reliable websites (e.g., www.pexels.com) where you can secure high-quality videos to embed into the slides of your presentation. In this instance, it's a video that plays in the background as you make a point or discuss a topic. For example, pay close attention to how Amin Toufani uses this feature at minute 23:30 during his lecture on exponential finance titled "Exonomics," which was presented as part of the Singularity University Summits.[26] It's different from a video or clip that you play for the audience as a complement to your presentation (e.g., a TED Talk or a clip). Be sure the clip you choose intuitively supports the point you are making and *helps* make your point, as opposed to distracting the listener. Likewise, be sure the video does not lag or show poorly in an online presentation (and if you are unsure about the internet speeds and capabilities of your attendees, you may want to forgo embedded videos; you don't want the video to freeze your presentation as you are speaking). We recommend that you:

- use this feature to add some variety; it can be a nice way to keep attendees engaged.
- ensure the video aligns with your overall theme and look.
- avoid videos if you have any hesitations about the internet connections of your participants.

Use of External Video

Video is an excellent way to engage the audience differently—especially to give you a momentary break and to shift the audience's focus onto something or someone else for a few minutes. However, the use of video adds complexity in an online presentation, and just as we mentioned with embedded videos above, the success of a video will depend on your internet connection (as well as participants' connections). The online meeting platform may lag, which can be perceived as unprofessional. In addition, the point of your video may be lost or missed, so you will need to ensure that you are adding explanation to the vid-eo and why you want participants to watch it. One option is to embed the link to the video in the chat so users can view the video on their own screens. Another option is to assign the video as pre-work or post-work. Finally, ensure that the video is the appropriate length, and check that your contact is comfortable with including it in the presentation; we have clients say, "15 minutes for a video clip is way too long for this group," "they have already seen it," and "don't show more than one clip." Checking in ahead of time will help you deliver on expectations.

Humorous Images or Videos

"I'm not funny" is a comment we often hear from presenters. The reality is that you can design humor into your deck; it's a great way to keep the audience engaged and on their toes, and also connects people with you. Perhaps it's a fair-use cartoon that emphasizes a point, a meme, or some other image that accentuates your message. The image may be ironic, sarcastic, satirical, self-deprecating, witty, or hyperbolic. Just ensure that the image(s) you choose is appropriate for the audience.

The Closing Slide

All too often, the closing slide contains one word: "Questions?" While this is a clear signpost that you have reached the end of your presentation and are ready to turn the conversation over to the audience, the slide is expected. And it's a little underwhelming. To end your presentation in a memorable way, design a strong closing slide. Provide a powerful image, tell a story, provide a quote, talk about a better future. If you are delivering a persuasive presentation, summarize your content and solidify the argument to prompt audience members to be ready to respond. Finish strong so the audience remembers you (in a positive way); remember how we discussed at the beginning of this book how we wonder what participants will say about our presentations the next day? Conclude in a way that makes attendees talk enthusiastically about what you presented, whether it's in the next hour, the next day, or the next week.

The Notes Section

The "notes" section of your slides (which should not be visible to attendees during your presentation) is a great place to keep your outline. The key word in the previous sentence is "outline." While it could be a helpful exercise for you to type in your notes word-for-word during your design and drafting process as a way to gather your thoughts and ideas and "practice," those full sentences and paragraphs should be whittled down to bullet points or fragments by the time your presentation arrives so they simply represent visual cues. In our experience, leaving full sentences and paragraphs in your notes is a recipe for disaster unless you are skilled at memorization. While we absolutely understand that speakers want to be prepared and ensure that they cover all of the most important information, we believe that having your presentation written out in front of you could become distracting...*for you*. We have seen nervous speakers read directly from their notes, or stop to reread the notes quickly to ensure that they covered everything before moving on. Resist the urge to use the notes as a crutch, and treat them as reminders for yourself.

Another way we have seen the notes used is by recording additional content that you would like attendees to access. Maybe this means source material, evidence, data, or background information. You do not necessarily need to address what is in the notes in this case; rather, it is something your audience members can view and be reminded of later. One final way that the notes can be used is to store backup data in case an audience member asks you a question (i.e., sales figures, dates, additional reading recommendations, etc.). Again, the content of these notes would not be necessary to talk about, but it's there if you happen to need it.

While this section focused on engaging PowerPoint slides, we have one final consideration. We were reminded by Eileen Sheil, Vice President of Communications at Medtronic, that sometimes, a slide deck is *not* the appropriate tool. She said to us, "Sometimes I think, 'Can we just have a discussion about something with an agenda, rather than another presentation?'" Ed Markey, Vice President of Corporate Communications at Goodyear Tire & Rubber Co., had a similar sentiment when he suggested, "The presenter has to be very judicious in how that material is used. Especially if it's going to be a longer presentation. You have to keep the audience engaged, and you don't want them to work. In other words, you don't want to put up a PowerPoint that has, you know, 600 words on it, and expect them to read it while you're talking." We could not agree more. Sometimes, another slide deck will just get lost in the mountain of other slide decks. On some occasions, *not* using a deck can set you apart.

Conclusion—Let Your Message Live

By carefully designing your slide deck and making critical decisions about how your images and text are organized and presented, you will eliminate unnecessary and distracting "slide clutter" and let your message live. Keep your message center stage and remove the noise and clutter—especially online, where people can "fade" more quickly than in person ("Zoom fatigue" is definitely real!). To continue with the home metaphor, if your structure is the foundation presented at the end of Chapter 2, your slide deck is the curb appeal. An engaging deck that complements and enhances your message is a win/win—a win for you, and a win for your audience as well.
In a nutshell, don't let a sound structure be ruined by a deck that is sloppy, busy, and unappealing to the audience...or is shoddily constructed and could collapse any minute.

Chapter 4 sets the stage for your delivery, and is all about designing your setting and technology. After a sound structure and a beautiful slide design, your setting and technology represent your first opportunity to engage with the audience. In fact, we would assert that *it's the new first impression.* What do your setting and technology communicate about you? Let's find out.

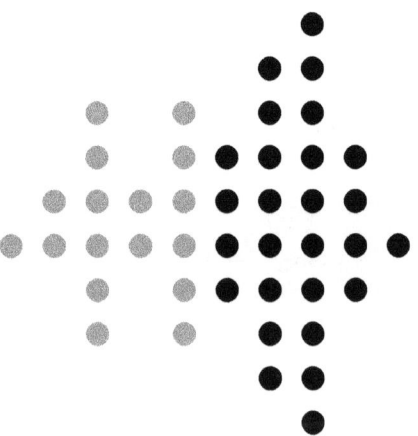

CHAPTER 4:
DESIGN YOUR SETTING & TECH

"Have you checked your audio levels? Your screen presentation? Have you checked your backgrounds? Your internet connection?"

—Ed Markey, Vice President of Corporate Communications at Goodyear Tire & Rubber Co.

Simply put, the setting for your online presentation is the new way to make a first impression, for better or worse. Toastmaster World Champion Aaron Beverly said when speaking to us about the importance of setting, "Your computer screen is your stage....you now have to think about how you can use the stage, but use it in a very limited square." With that, you have to remember that as opposed to entering another person or organization's space to present in-person, when you are giving an online presentation, you are letting participants into your space. Thus, you need to think about what will show up around and behind you. It's a lot to think about! Think about or take a look around at your normal "work space," and imagine that your webcam is on right now (bonus points if you actually turn on your webcam to test it out while you're reading this). Take inventory: is your space well-lit, interesting, and professional? Or are you a shadowy figure on the couch with a ceiling fan running in the background? Are audience members looking up your nose? Or are you parallel with the camera? Are you looking off to the side for the entire presentation, or are you square with the camera? Does your internet speed meet the challenge, or is it constantly going in and out? What is appearing in the background? Are the audience members going to be focused on your vintage concert poster collection covering the wall behind you, or are they seeing a minimally-decorated setting? The reality is that there are several technology- and space-oriented considerations for anyone hoping to succeed when presenting online.

Presenting online requires that you think intentionally about a number of dimensions—and in some cases, you may need to invest in some equipment or supplies to ensure that you present your best self online. Designing a home setup that is professional and best complements your brand is an investment. Brandon Charpied, Executive Director of the Management & Organizational Behavior Teaching Society, said, "In total, I personally spent $2,500 to ensure my organizations could provide the online environments that would assist in our members being able to engage without technological limitations during our conferences." On the other end of the spectrum, Scott spent about $600 on a microphone, webcam, headphones, green screen, and shelving. We certainly are not trying to spend your money, and we understand that funds may not always be readily available to create this ideal setup; rather, we aim to present you with ideas and recommendations to show you what these purchases could add to your environment. Further, Scott and Brandon each view these upgrades as an investment—in their personal brands, and the brands of their organizations.

We strongly recommend planning for each element that we describe in this chapter, and then recording a dry run to ensure you are conveying the desired image.

Setting & Space

Your space should be clean, warm, and well-lit (which helps you look good, according to the article *How to Look Good on Camera, According to Tom Ford*).[27] People tend to go one way or the other here, plopping down in front of the whitest wall in their house or setting up in the middle of their messy kitchen (or a clothes closet, or even a bathroom... and yes, we have seen people presenting online in both of those settings). As you choose your space, you need to think about the first impression you would like to make. Finally, make sure the camera is parallel with your eyes, and well-spaced from your face. Figure 1 depicts a number of different laptop placements and speaker postures; the image in the second row, on the right, represents the ideal laptop placement and corresponding speaker posture. In Figure 2, various arrangements of a desktop computer are shown; all would work in relation to a speaker's posture.

Figure 1
Ideal Laptop Computer Placement—Image at Bottom Right

Figure 2
Ideal Desktop Computer Placement—All Four Images Work

Minimizing Tech Distractions

Scott has a short checklist that he goes through prior to an online presentation. Essentially, he shuts down all unneeded programs (e.g., Microsoft Word, Google Docs) and applications (e.g., calendar, email), and silences his phone. Not only does this clear away "noise" and distraction, it spares listeners from hearing chirps and dings as texts, emails, and phone calls come pouring in. The impact of making the mistake of not minimizing distractions was captured by Andrew Ziemba, Program & Licensing Manager at MTD Products, when he stated, "A rookie mistake on my part was I did not silence my phone. My Ring doorbell app was going off during the presentation. Not only was this distracting for me, but one executive thought this was part of the presentation and noted how this did not work for her." Think of it this way: if it's going to be distracting for *you*, then it will become a distraction for *everyone else*.

Location

Scott has spent the last few months working out of a guest bedroom in his basement. He spent $300 at Target and had some shelving and a desk delivered. The guest bed was pushed into a corner of the room, and thankfully no one can see the cardboard boxes upon which his laptop sits to ensure the camera is at eye level. Unless you have the time and energy to completely renovate a space, it's likely that, like Scott, you will have to improvise.

However, the basement room provides Scott with privacy and it is a quiet space in his house from which to hold class, deliver presentations, and work. If possible, choose a location that affords you some quiet and privacy. We understand that this can be challenging, and that it may be considered a luxury for some people to have a spare bedroom or even a home office to work in, but you would be surprised what you can create out of a corner nook or an unused space in your apartment or home. And if space is limited for you, choose an area where you can close a door or muffle any distractions from other rooms—and then position yourself in the part of that area where your body blocks out beds, shelves, or anything else that you cannot move or put away.

Dress

Some research has found that wearing new clothes can put you in a good mood.[28] We've observed a significant shift in norms around dress for online presentations. In a general sense, it seems that even in corporate life, business casual attire is more and more acceptable. While dressing for presentations is outside of our scope, we would suggest having a conversation about the appropriate dress as you plan and coordinate with your supervisor or organizational contact. It's best to have this conversation and dress slightly above than be under-dressed and too casual.

In addition to clarifying norms, it is critical that you check your outfit with your lighting and your background before going live. Scott witnessed a presentation where the speaker wore a black top, had a dark background, and their lighting rendered half of their face a shadow. Not only was this distracting, but it also communicated a lack of awareness and professionalism, and in Scott's eyes, it diminished the speaker's credibility. Maria viewed a presentation where the speaker was sitting in front of patterned curtains, and was also wearing a shirt that had a different pattern in a color scheme that clashed with the curtains. The "loudness" of the curtains and the clothing pattern overtook any virtual attendee's ability to focus on the speaker and, sadly, was visually overwhelming. If you are unable to control the background colors or patterns in your presenting space, offset that with what you choose to wear.

We were struck by an honest and impactful comment made by Micki Byrnes, President & General Manager at WKYC-TV, who was commenting on a colleague that caught her eye (in a good way). Micki commented, "She looks very appropriately dressed for the occasion...always just a click above everybody else. And it makes an excellent impression versus the people who look like hell." This suggests to us that people who do spend time thinking about every aspect of their appearance make a stronger impression on participants, and we believe that the time that goes into that preparation is worth it.

Lighting

When you appear on the screen, are you a shadowy figure nestled on a couch where only one side of your face is illuminated, or does the light around you (whether natural or artificial) help make your entire face easily visible? Or, as Ed Markey, Vice President of Corporate Communications at Goodyear Tire & Rubber Co. said, "Are you back sort of in the ether somewhere?" Depending on your objectives, lighting is a critical component of your presentation, and is another important element that contributes to professionalism.

In online presentations that we have watched, we have noted a number of common mistakes that should be considered before your presentation. While natural light is important, where that is in relation to you makes a difference; if the light is shining directly behind you, it will drown you out and your audience will have trouble seeing you clearly. Likewise, half a window or lighting on just one side can be problematic as well because only half of your face will be lit. Another common mistake is relying on lighting from a ceiling fan—which can be extremely distracting for your audience, especially when the fan is running. Finally, for readers who wear glasses, test the glare; on more than one occasion, we have found ourselves staring at a presenter with glowing eyes (caused by reflections from their computer screen). Likewise, test your lighting—sometimes we see the frames, but not a speaker's eyes, which is difficult to watch for an hour.

In her article, *How to Look Your Best on a Webcam*,[29] Julie Lasky warns "never to sit directly under a light source; it will throw under-eye and next-to-nose shadows. A lamp or window positioned two feet directly opposite to you that lights you evenly will be most flattering and will not cast glare on your screen." So when you are designing your setting, test your lighting, especially at different times of the day. Another consideration (particularly if you give presentations or lead meetings frequently) is to purchase a lighting system. This approach ensures that your lighting is reliable and consistent regardless. Online retailers offer several options, from ring lights for cell phones or tablets, Lumecube for laptops, to softbox lighting systems with stands. You can even purchase webcams with built-in lighting systems for laptops or PCs.

Your Background

"Background" here refers to two different categories (computer-generated and natural), and with both, we are referring to what is behind you in your workspace. While some presenters are comfortable with their camera view including whatever is in their workspace, some others choose a virtual background that hides the contents of their physical location. So in this section, that is what we mean by "background." Your background—what appears behind you, whether it is a virtual image or real content—is a critical consideration that should be given significant attention. What do you want to communicate? Are you huddled in a closet? Are you a shadowy figure that moves in and out of the beach-themed Zoom background? Are you in a bedroom with white walls and grandma's quilt in the background? Are you at your poorly lit kitchen table with people wandering around in the background? Ultimately, we suggest being intentional about the image you want to portray.

Computer-Generated Backgrounds – Computer-generated backgrounds are a good option when you do not feel confident in your natural background (e.g., you *need* to present from your kitchen). When using the computer-generated backgrounds, it's best to do so with a green screen set up behind you, since some computer models require a certain operating system to allow a background *without* a green screen. Green screen backdrops cost $15-20, and complete systems are sold for close to $50. Using a green screen will render you and your background image crisp, clean, and clear. And you will not move in and out of focus like a ghostly figure. Keep in mind, though, the "personality" of the image that you choose; we have seen everything from lush apartment balconies in Paris to the campus football field to a bingo board, which are suitable for casual meetings, but could be distracting in a professional setting. A final consideration is to be sure your background communicates professionalism; the whiskey bottle you used for your last virtual happy hour may not be appropriate for your Monday morning check-in.

Natural Backgrounds – Natural backgrounds require several considerations—the most important of which is, "What do I want to communicate by using this background?" In a general sense, you want your background to communicate something about you: what pictures, paintings, books, and knick-knacks will best represent you? This is

DESIGN YOUR SETTING & TECH

a personal question that only you can answer, but you do want to remember that participants *will* be looking at what else is on the screen around and behind you.

It's also important to consider the following mistakes we have witnessed during the transition to online presentations:

- Poorly lit spaces, or spaces that are too bright; in both instances, the presenter's face is not clearly visible.
- Clothes closets, corners, and anything that resembles a bunker.
- Ceiling fans in your background, where the movement becomes distracting and light gets obstructed (the same goes for horizontal blinds, which can block the light in a patterned way).
- Controversial images, items, or artifacts—political posters, etc.
- Odd camera angles (e.g., diagonals). Position your face square with the camera and even with your eyes.
- Cluttered or messy spaces that leave your audience reading everything written on the whiteboard and Post-It notes covering the walls behind you, or trying to find where you are amidst all the piles of "stuff."

Desk/Seating

Choose a chair that is not rickety and if you choose a chair that swivels, be sure that you are not unconsciously swiveling back and forth for the entire meeting—the equivalent of the meeting participant who cannot stop fidgeting. Variations of swiveling are rocking and bouncing. Avoid presenting from your couch, La-Z-Boy recliner, or bar stool, too; in essence, if you wouldn't sit in or on it during an in-person seminar or presentation, don't do so when you are *giving* the presentation! In addition, ensure that you have easy access to your mouse or keyboard so you can advance slides without making a big deal of pausing, leaning forward, and clicking.

Perhaps most importantly, your computer's webcam should be square with you as the presenter and at eye level (see the diagram presented in the Setting & Space section of this chapter). Think of yourself as a newscaster—just as newscasters appear to be sitting across your living room and talking with you eye-to-eye, you should be even with the camera and looking directly into the eye of it. As Carol Kinsey Goman suggests in her article, *Body Language Hacks to Project Leadership*,[30] "The best tip for looking confident in a virtual meeting is to sit with good posture—facing the screen with shoulders squared, head straight, and feet flat on the ground." We witness too many people who miss this important element and as a result, we are looking up their noses or they are looking off to the side for the entire presentation.

A Concise List of Miscellaneous Pro Tips

- Silence your phone (or put it in another room).
- Shut down all other apps and programs on your computer.
- Even if your battery is at 100%, plug the power cord in to avoid unexpected shutdowns or worrying about constantly checking your battery meter throughout the presentation.
- Record a practice session prior to your presentation and have a coworker or loved one give you feedback on your setting and space (Maria once helped a friend configure the perfect place in an apartment to do an interview via Skype, and it was a helpful exercise for moving chairs, trying lights on or lights off, and positioning the computer screen).

Technological Considerations

Internet Connection

"I've learned that ethernet connection is a lot better than Wi-Fi connection. I connected my router to my computer because the connection speed is critical."

—Aaron Beverly, 2019 Toastmasters
World Champion of Public Speaking

"My internet connection is slow" will only last as an excuse for a little while longer. We anticipate that many of you who are reading this have heard colleagues and other professionals use this excuse for months. There are four primary considerations: an ethernet cable, your plan, your modem, and your family. The *best* path forward is to plug your computer directly into your router. Along with a hard connection, contact your internet provider and clarify your high-speed internet plan. One consideration is to switch your plan. In his article, *The Dos and Donts of Online Meetings*,[31] Brian Chen suggests, "If your speeds are below 20 megabits per second, there's a high likelihood your video is going to look pixelated and have audio delays." To verify your current speed, you can visit the website http://speedtest.net. Another option is to update your modem/router and ensure that yours is designed for the internet plan you have chosen. A final consideration is to have everyone in your home switch their electronic devices to Airplane Mode. That should also mean that no one is streaming content or playing video games. These three simple adjustments can ensure that technology is one less concern when presenting online.

Presentation Security

While not a primary focus of our book, we were reminded of the importance of security. This may be important to explore with your host, or if you are in control of the session, ensure that you have required a password for attendees to enter. There have been plenty of "Zoom bombing" reports in the media and Brandon Charpied, Executive Director of the Management & Organizational Behavior Teaching Society, underscored the impact of these incidents when he told us:

> While we have all heard stories of horrible Zoom bombing experiences, I am aware of four utterly horrific experiences that were far worse than what often gets reported in the media. Three of [these] were experienced by close friends, one [...] occurred in my own household. This left an incredible impression—and fear, quite honestly—of how I would protect my constituents across many thousands of interactions online....Not only can an unsafe and unsecure environment be damaging to an isolated presentation, but it can be damaging to one's career, one's institution, and more.

Computer/Laptop

"My laptop is so old" is another excuse we have heard over and over in recent months. While we understand that not everyone can afford new technology, there are some accessible options that will work better than your 7-year-old laptop. In some cases, a $300 Chromebook will work much better than hardware that is old and not compatible with other technology. If your livelihood depends on your ability to present online, ensuring that you have the right technology for the work is a critical consideration.

Multiple Screens/Monitors

Speakers with two screens/monitors often over-rely on their second screen to read or review the "notes" section of their slide deck. We suggest avoiding this technique because it draws your eyes away from the camera and to the other screen. Recall that in this medium, "eye contact" means you are looking into the camera eye, as opposed to at a screen.

Sound—Headsets

When it comes to sound quality, Aaron Beverly, 2019 Toastmasters World Champion of Public Speaking, said it best: "People will be turned off more if you have bad sound." If you are using your computer's audio to present, it can create a cavernous effect—especially if you are in a bigger room, or a room with wood floors. Your audience needs to hear the best version of you and we suggest, at a minimum, using a headset with a microphone that you can plug into your desktop/laptop. Other options include Apple EarPods, which have a wire and a Lightning Port connector, or devices similar to Apple AirPods, which are wireless. When choosing a headset, there are a few important considerations. People with long hair will want to choose a system that will not be compromised by that (or keep your hair behind your shoulders or ears, away from the earpiece and microphone). We have witnessed several presenters choose systems where their hairstyle interfered with the sound (e.g., strands of hairs brushing past the microphone). And while it can seem trivial, it's important to consider the image you want to convey. Do you want to look like a gamer, an air traffic controller, or a millennial?

Using an external microphone is another option—especially if online presentations are a significant part of your role. There are several "good" options that will do the job. Popular choices are Blue Yeti, ATR2100, or Snowball. For those who want to learn more, an online search will quickly provide you with a number of options to best suit your needs.

Webcams

For presenters who use webcams that are separate devices from the webcam built into a laptop (or on laptops where the webcam lens is not on the top of the screen), the most common problem we notice is that the individual's webcam is not square with their face. Rather, it's located somewhere else so that when they present, they appear to be looking off to the side. So if you plan to use a separate High Definition (HD 1080) webcam, we suggest that you mount the webcam square with your face, as though you are a newscaster. If you are using a webcam that is part of a laptop, be sure the laptop is at 90 degrees, and at eye level. This might mean that you stack your laptop on a few books like Scott does. We were impressed when we read Ivan Buzarin's piece *How to Prep for Speaking at a Virtual Conference*, and would highly recommend that you take some time to review his article.[32]

Conclusion—Milliseconds Matter

In a study about first impressions, the authors found that "people base their first impressions of others on whatever information is available within the first 39 milliseconds."[33] Another study found that it's 100 milliseconds.[34] That's milliseconds. Admittedly, these are only two studies, and they were not conducted in the context of online presentations, but these still represent important data points—and ones that we feel are incredibly important (and a little astounding). *You and your setting* are now intertwined and included in the equation. During the process of writing this book, we have seen some pretty odd "stages." We witnessed senior executives conduct meetings from their bathroom (yes, this actually did happen), laundry room, closet, or back deck, and even had participants attend from their (moving) cars. Without venturing too deep into the topic of personal brand, we feel that these "meeting locations" deserve a mention. The setting and your technology matter—

so does an immediate smile while the audience sizes up you and your setting in a few milliseconds.

Speaking of smiling, it's showtime in Chapter 5. At this point, you have practiced audience-centered design, built a solid structure, designed an engaging deck, and created a "stage" that is on-brand. You also have the tech to support your work, or have some ideas of what you want to order. We briefly explore anxiety and the importance of setting the emotional tone. We also examine several topics associated with verbal and nonverbal dimensions of your actual presentation. This is the final stop on the road to mastering the online presentation.

CHAPTER 5:
DESIGN YOUR DELIVERY

"People who just have that spark and can look through the screen and they know they're talking to people, just like them. They have a sense of their worth and they are comfortable in their skin. They know they're adding value and the content translates to you in a way that you understand. Perhaps a little bit self-deprecating, and you know they want that connection with you to be real."

—Micki Byrnes,
President & General Manager at WKYC-TV

The ultimate goal from a delivery standpoint is to present yourself as professional, authentic, and accessible. We have all worked with people who are professional, but lack accessibility (presidential candidates Bob Dole and John Kerry suffered from this reality at times).

When actually delivering the presentation, pay close attention to the audience; there is one simple question that can help you gauge your performance. The question Scott asks himself is, "Am I good enough to keep them off their devices?" Are all the pieces—structure, content, slides, technology, delivery—in concert? If so, you are more likely to connect, have an impact, and—depending on your objectives—inspire action.

Great *delivery* of a presentation is like watching a world-class orchestra in action. Each piece of the whole is perfectly timed, aligned, and executed at near perfection—certainly as the result of many hours of rehearsal, both rough and fine-tuned. As you read the following passage, keep the orchestra metaphor in mind. When all of these elements of the presentation are perfectly timed, aligned, and executed well, the presenter will connect at a much deeper level than those who are missing even one or two of these elements. For example, a presenter may have incredible content, and 90% of the elements locked in, but their slow pace, lack of vocal variety, and infrequent eye contact diminish their ability to connect. It would be like listening to the "William Tell Overture" without the bass drum, cymbals, and the piccolo. Regardless of how all of those other instruments perform, the piece of music would not connect in the same way.

The good news is this. It's likely that 70% of the items listed in the following section are not an issue for you. Some of you reading this book expertly use your voice, maintain eye contact, and don't struggle with rocking or swaying. However, if you are like us, you *do* have 3-4 items that are opportunities for growth. And when we identify them, work through them, and bring them to a place of unconscious competence (see Chapter 6), it's as if the bass drum has been reintroduced to the piece of music.

Addressing Anxiety/Nerves

"I was definitely nervous. My heart was racing. My adrenaline was super high. I had to think about what was making me anxious. I was about to go on stage for the World Championship of Public Speaking in front of about 2000 people. I had to get that out of my head. I had to focus not on the contest, but on the matter at hand, which was my speech."

—Aaron Beverly, 2019 Toastmasters World Champion of Public Speaking

The technical term for presentation anxiety is glossophobia. Nerves impact even the most experienced speakers, including Aaron Beverly and the authors of this book. In the most nervous moments, it's easy to allow negative self-talk to swallow both you and your ability to focus. Though it may take some time, we believe that moving from the self-disparaging comments that characterize a fixed mindset (e.g., "I am not good, can't get better, and don't enjoy giving presentations") to the more positive, reaffirming ones that accompany a growth mindset (e.g., "I am not where I want to be...*yet*") is a transformative process that requires commitment and investment. Putting in the effort and working toward becoming more and more comfortable is an identity shift—but in the end, is worth the time.

The good news is that we have seen the shift begin to occur within several hours. We've worked with hundreds of people who have moved from "I can't" to "wow, maybe I can!" The topic of nerves has been discussed extensively in other volumes on public speaking and we have created a list of experiments you can run to see what works best for you in the Appendix. However, there are a few considerations for presenting in an online environment that can minimize anxiety.

If you have not done so before, try traditional approaches to navigating nerves that have been well-explored in the literature on presentations (e.g., visualization, skills training, rational emotive therapy).[35] Second, do your best to ensure that all aspects of technology are set up, connected, and working as they should be—sound, internet connection, lighting, and so forth. Third, manage your environment to the best of your ability; ask your partner to take the kids on a bike ride, ensure family members are off their devices (i.e., maximize your bandwidth), or plant yourself in a quiet and secluded location. A fourth recommendation is to design your environment; yes, we did talk about designing your setting earlier, but here we mean finding ways to *personalize* it, to create comfort and motivation. Maybe it's a sticky note that says "Smile!" as a reminder, a photo of your family next to the computer, a glass of water, or a cup of coffee. Our final suggestion is to keep your presentation crisp and clean. If getting through the presentation is a heavy lift for you, *imagine how your audience feels*.

Setting the Emotional Tone

Presenting from a podium is much different than a TED Talk. In a similar vein, presenting online is different than being in front of a live audience. When presenting online, *you* are responsible for establishing the emotional tone and serving as the "spark." A core task of a speaker is setting the best emotional tone. This means that you use *yourself* to alter the emotional state of individuals in the audience, moving them in the desired direction. Setting the emotional tone means that you are neither underwhelming nor overwhelming. You hit just the right tone for the group in front of you. For instance, an overly enthusiastic presentation to a group of engineers may miss the mark because they may expect a more formal, in formative, balanced presentation. However, a typical engineer in front of a group of nurses could miss the mark as well.

So how do you know if you have hit the right tone? Look to the screens of your participants. Are they wide-eyed and smiling, or are their heads down and focused on something else? Are they laughing and enjoying their time, or do they look like they would rather be elsewhere? The data is in front of you ninety-nine percent of the time. Pay close attention, and if need be, switch up the energy by using humor, storytelling, a chat discussion, or a small group interaction. Ryan Franks, Business Manager at Energy Storage Response Group, told us about a hack he uses to remind himself about setting and maintaining the correct tone. He said, "I affix a note near my camera that contained two reminder words, 'act' and 'energy,' to remind myself to do those things throughout the delivery."

There are simple, tried and true ways to set the tone, even before you begin. We cannot express the importance of this enough—if you set a positive, energizing, and uplifting tone, you will win the audience over from the beginning. If you do the opposite, you will be digging out of a difficult situation as you try and win participants back. The following list is designed to provide you with some techniques for doing so.

Music – Scott always begins with music. If you choose to do this, are you playing some old-school Motown, or a Bach piece being played on the harpsichord? Each of these musical selections would set a different tone for the day. Scott always asks the first few people tuning in what they would like to listen to (and their answers could give you some clues about the audience members, or even the organization). On one occasion, a woman told Scott that she would like to listen to "TV theme songs," and they laughed for a long time before that session began. Another time, a participant requested "Yacht Rock," which is a genre that Scott had never heard of. In this instance, the participant's answer, as well as the music that was discovered, had everyone in the session laughing. As you can see, music can set a tone for a session. It may not be appropriate for every occasion, but if you *do* use music, think to yourself first: What tone do you want to set?

Smile (specifically, a Duchenne Smile[36]) – A presenter's smile is one important way to set the emotional tone. However, there are multiple kinds of smiles. One is a fake smile, and the other is a Duchenne smile. What distinguishes the Duchenne smile is that it involves the eyes. In other words, the eyes light up as well, and the muscles around the eyes "crinkle." Communications expert Larry Morrow calls this "smiling with your eyes." A smile into the eyes of your participants even before you begin (e.g., while you are being introduced) can set a tone that will serve you well. Fake smiles and inauthentic energy/enthusiasm are counterproductive, and participants will see through those easily and become disengaged.

Engage/Build Relationships – If possible, spend some time chatting with participants so you have a chance to get comfortable, build relationships, and learn a little about them. Scott has had wonderful luck using this technique; similar to the way asking the first few participants to arrive what their musical tastes are, just taking some time to casually chat provides you with data you can use during the presentation, or helps you better understand examples that will resonate. In addition, you may learn a little more about the organization, its function, or participants' hopes for the session.

The Screen – Participants can enter into a quiet room with a blank screen, or they can log into a learning experience. One option is to have scrolling facts, data, statistics, quotes, cartoons, or visuals that help set the tone for the day. You could also give participants a task to help get them into the mindset; Scott once had a group "draw leadership" while they waited for everyone else to arrive. He used these in his intro and it was fun and interesting because it gave the group a common starting point that he referred back to.

Delivery—Time

You do not want to be the person who goes past their allotted time—especially in the era of "Zoom fatigue," when so many people may have multiple online meetings back-to-back in one day. Whether it's with a C-Suite leader, a pitch for potential business, or your college professor, you need to stay within the allotted time boundaries. This means that you have an intense focus on time and you have a system in place to monitor this dimension of your talk. Perhaps you set the timer on your phone or tap an audience member to provide you with pre-established signals from the audience to monitor how many minutes are left, or when you have reached the point where you had wanted to move to Q & A, an activity, or something else. When it comes to time, we are reminded of a quote by Franklin D. Roosevelt, former president of the United States: "Be sincere; be brief; be seated." In the year 2020 (and beyond), we know the first two are still relevant!

Delivery—Multiple Presenters

If you are engaging with multiple panelists who are pre-planned into your presentation, it is your responsibility to somehow "signal" when they are expected to speak, and you may want to ask them before the presentation to find a way to indicate that they have finished their answer or contribution, perhaps by calling on the next presenter or saying something like "that is how I see it from my experience." Maria has been in multiple meetings and webinars where there are a number of presenters who do not clearly indicate the end of their information, and then there is awkward silence before someone asks, "Oh is it my turn now?" or "Are you done speaking, Jen? I wasn't sure." The other instinct, when there is no effort to transition smoothly between speakers, is that multiple people begin speaking at once, which creates even more awkwardness and time loss. So if you have multiple speakers, here are some helpful tips:

- If you're planning a panel discussion with multiple questions, come up with an order of respondents. Either follow the same order for each question, or say "We'll start with George on this one" after you have asked the question.
- Indicate to the audience when you will be bringing in the panelists, and when their contributions are complete.
- Ensure if you can that the primary video is on the person who is speaking (or mention to the audience that they can select a function like "Speaker View" on Zoom to automatically highlight the speaker).

Delivery—Verbal

Balancing Memorization & Notes

Two common presentation practices are to memorize your presentation or to use notes exclusively. The best approach is a balance of the two. Memorize your outline, maybe an important quote, and then simply fill in the blanks for your listeners. You may also use your slide to remind you of significant points. Remember that the slides in your presentation should only serve as an outline and not contain too much content. *Is there anything worse than a presenter reading you their slide deck word for word?!* It's a perfect recipe for people to check out, become disengaged, and feel like prisoners. It's also a great opportunity for participants to turn to other tasks—especially online.

> *"An online meeting gives participants the opportunity not to listen."*
>
> —Marc Gillinov, MD, Chair of the Department of Thoracic & Cardiovascular Surgery at Cleveland Clinic

Unless you are in a context where it's the norm do so (e.g., speech and debate), do not read your presentation. This is a surefire way to lose people. Christina Cashin, Senior Vice President of Talent Management at KeyBank, expressed frustration when she found herself stuck in a session where the presenter was reading from a script. She commented, "Just send me the script and I'll read it myself…people who drone on and read from scripts have not packaged their information well." Avoid essentially giving your audience permission to check out by talking extemporaneously as much as possible, using your well-designed slides and minimal notes as springboards.

When presenting online, too many notes will take your eye contact from the camera, and you may find yourself looking down too much. Looking down or away once in a while is normal, but when a speaker spends 30 to 50% of their time reading or looking away from the camera, it's a missed opportunity to connect and a ripe opportunity for listeners to move on to multitask.

Setting a Conversational Tone

Great communicators connect with their audience. Maggie Mills, 2020 National Champion of Public Forum Debate in the National Speech and Debate Association, emphasized the importance of this connection—and its audience impact—when she told us, "We were talking more conversationally, [which] made our actual delivery of speeches more appealing." A conversational or accessible tone can help a speaker connect and relate to the audience. This does not mean the speaker lacks professionalism; the goal is to be professional *and* accessible. A conversational tone means that you communicate in a way that is not overly perfect, memorized, or rehearsed. Few attendees want to listen to a perfect, plastic, robot person. Setting a conversational tone lets the audience get to know *you*.

That said, you may find that you have to adjust your "in-person" approach when you are presenting, especially if you are involving the audience in ways where they would be responding to your questions, offering ideas, or sharing opinions. As we have mentioned so far, it's easy for online sessions to drag on, or for people to talk over each other when norms and expectations are not established. Marc Gillinov, MD alluded to this when he said that as he started leading more meetings online, he found himself becoming more assertive: "I wouldn't do this in person, but I *dominated* the meeting." We are not suggesting here that you need to change your personality, becoming more formal and less conversational or lighthearted; what we *do* mean is that you may need to drive the presentation and its components with a bit more assertiveness than you would if you were leading an in-person session.

Helping You Shine Through—Professional & Accessible

From a delivery standpoint, a challenge for each of us is to strike a balance of authenticity and professionalism. Another way to say it is, are you professional *and* accessible? Participants want to get to know you—a professional version of you. This can be a difficult balance. At times presenters come across as technically perfect, but also robotic. Other times, their authenticity shines through, but in a less than professional manner. On this front, Maggie Mills and her debate partner, Sasha Haines, shared a few comments that stood out to us:

- "We knew that we prepared well, and we were having a lot of fun. So we went into each round and we had the mindset of 'Okay, whether we win or whether we lose, we're here. We're having fun, it's fine.' And then we did really, really well at that tournament."

- "Simultaneously being ourselves and doing what feels comfortable and having a good time with it makes it exponentially easier as well as more enjoyable to watch."

Each of the statements hints at the balance Maggie and Sasha intentionally struck between being well-prepared and professional, and displaying their authentic selves. In our opinion, they are wise beyond their years. Scott will often use a Wi-Fi metaphor when discussing this topic (see Image 3 below).

Image 3

What's Your Signal Strength?

He explains that you, the presenter, are the circle at the bottom, and your goal is to connect at full signal strength. We all know what it feels like when connectivity is poor. It's frustrating. Poor connectivity with a presenter is equally frustrating. Here's how the metaphor works. Again, place yourself as the circle looking out at the bands. When we work with a presenter who displays:

- *one bar of signal strength* – the presenter is often so consumed with their nerves and "just getting through" that they can do little else than make their body go through the motions.
- *two bars of signal strength* – the presenter manages their nerves well, and may even be a good presenter, but there's something missing. They are going through the motions, but not connecting at full signal strength. It's quite like watching an automaton; you are not sure who the person is in there.
- *three bars of signal strength* – the presenter has overcome their nerves, is technically proficient, and their soul, personality, and sense of humor shine through. They are comfortable in their own skin and have a nice balance between humility and confidence.

What's the goal? For each one of us, it's having the ability to present at full signal strength. Of course, there may be times and contexts where two bars is the appropriate level. Your personality and sense of humor are not what's important. What is important is that *you have the ability* to move between the two, and to do so with great skill.

Even for tried-and-true professionals, though, there is a learning curve in getting to a point where you truly understand how well you are connecting in an online environment. We are reminded of the words of Lillian Powell, Accountant at Defense Finance and Accounting Service, who reflected, "There is a difference in presenting to an audience face-to-face versus using an online platform. I could not determine how well I connected with the audience." Her statement underscores the importance of obtaining honest and authentic feedback so any speaker, novice or professional, better understands how well they are connecting online.

Transitional Phrases

Adding transitional phrases in between thoughts or slides (or even between segments of an online presentation, like when the speaker is shifting to a screen-share) can help soften the speaker and will eliminate awkward pauses in between slides. Transitional phrases help you bring listeners into your story.[37] For instance, "along with X, Y, & Z, it's important to remember that…" or "another interesting finding was that…" will help with transitioning between slides. When you are going to share your screen, you can indicate that by simply saying "I'm now going to share my screen so we can all look at this document together" (instead of silence and then asking "Can you see my screen?", which we hear often). These phrases can serve as bridges from one concept to another and provide listeners an opportunity to transition *with* you. They will also demonstrate your confidence as you move through the elements of your presentation, as opposed to being befuddled or unsure of how the technology works.

Be aware, though. At times, the speaker defaults to words like "so," "and," "I mean," and "you know" as a way to start new sentences. Like everything, the keys are intentionality and moderation. A few of these are not a problem, but we have witnessed speakers begin almost 50% of their sentences with "So…".

Oral Signposts

Oral signposts help listeners follow along. In essence, you are taking the audience on a tour and letting them know where you are going, what they are seeing, who is speaking (if there are multiple panelists), and where they have been. The classic phrase is to "tell them what you are going to tell them, tell them, tell them what you told them." Oral signposts are verbal indicators for where you and the audience are in the process. Here are some of the most common signposts:

- Beginning/Introduction – "I am going to begin today with a story," or "I am going to begin our discussion with a startling statistic…"
- Roadmap/Agenda/Outline – "The outline for my presentation is quick and simple; first…" or "Today's agenda looks like this…" or "The outline of my presentation is as follows."
- Body of the Presentation – "My first principle is X," "We've explored X and my second principle is Y," or "X & Y were the first two principles and Z is my third."
- Shifting to Another Speaker – "I would like to introduce X, who will be talking more about their experience with this topic. X, I'll let you take over."
- Return to Roadmap/Agenda/Outline – "Today we have discussed X, Y, and Z," or "At the beginning of our time together, I mentioned the agenda would include a discussion of X, Y, and Z," or "To recap…"
- Conclusion – "To summarize, please remember this important data point," or "I am going to conclude with a story," or "let me conclude with a picture of what our future could be…"

Oral Citations

Critical in the world of speech and debate and in instances where you are "citing" an expert resource, it's critical to cite your source. Oral citations communicate that you are not just winging it – rather, your argument is built upon solid research. Oral citations are similar to oral signposts. They signal expertise to listeners. Some common oral citations include the following:

according to, and I quote, argues that, as reported, dated, explained, explains, goes on to say, had this to say, I quote, quote, quoted, reported by, reported that, reports, reports that, said, says, stated, states, writes that, and wrote that.

Be sure that your quotes, as well as your citations, are contextualized smoothly into your presentation, and onto your slides, so that listeners understand why they are being incorporated and why they are significant.

Word Choice—Emotion

"Throughout human history, our greatest leaders and thinkers have used the power of words to transform our emotions, to enlist us in their causes, and to shape the course of destiny. Words can not only create emotions, they create actions. And from our actions flow the results of our lives."

—Tony Robbins, speaker

The words you choose to use (and not use) are critical and can make or break your talk. The *Atlas of Emotions* (www.atlasofemotions.org), developed by world-renowned emotions scholar Paul Ekman, can help you think through the concept of emotion and key words to communicate sentiment. It's pretty fascinating! For instance, if you are attempting to energize, do your *words* evoke a positive emotional state? Or, if you are attempting to persuade the audience, are you using keywords that accentuate the strengths and/or benefits of your approach? The words you choose are critical. And, *how* they are delivered can be just as important. For instance, are you **bolding** or <u>underlining</u> the keywords with your voice? This is also called *emphasis*, which is the manner in which you stress or accent keywords. The use of emphasis is crucial to your words "landing" on the audience. Depending on your objective, the words you choose will add color, texture, and a vivid picture. So what words match your objective? Here are some examples of words that can powerfully communicate specific emotions:

- *Sadness* – anguish, sorrow, grief, despair, misery, hopelessness, helplessness, resignation, distraught, discouraged, disappointed
- *Fear* – terror, horror, panic, desperation, dread, anxiety, nervousness, trepidation
- *Disgust* – loathing, abhorrence, revulsion, repugnant, distaste, aversion, dislike
- A*nger* – fury, vengeful, bitter, argumentative, exasperation, frustration, annoyance
- *Enjoyment* – wonder, excitement, pride, peace, relief, amusement, compassion, joy, rejoicing
- *Gratitude* – appreciate, thankful, gratitude, thank you, grateful, indebted

In addition to choosing specific words and emphasizing them with your voice, pausing after key words could be another way to highlight their importance. Perhaps you want to share something poignant and then take a moment to let the sentiment "sink in" with the audience; if that's the case, add a brief pause and step back for a moment, looking around the screen at the audience members before moving on.

"The right word may be effective, but no word was ever as effective as a rightly timed pause."
—Mark Twain, author

Word Choice—Inclusion

The words and themes you choose can impact your audience in many ways. We were reminded of this by Micki Byrnes, President & General Manager at WKYC-TV, who described the following about a session she attended: "The presentation was definitely male-oriented and the speaker's background was sports or whatever. And he talked like he was talking to a locker room full of football players. I was taken aback by how over-the-top he was." In this instance, Micki indicates that the speaker did not fully consider everyone who might be in his audience, and thus constructed a presentation and spoke in a tone that seemed directed only toward one sector of the audience—thus alienating the rest of the listeners. To demonstrate that you have *every* audience member in mind, we reinforce our assertion that it's critical to be intentional about your themes, visuals, and choice of words because they can unite, enthuse, and inspire, or divide, discourage, and exclude. Thus, it's critical that you choose your words with care and be as intentionally inclusive as possible.

In addition to many of the slang or racial slurs (both outdated and those still used today) that are inappropriate and unprofessional for formal presentations, some phrases should be avoided as well. In the United States, common phrases like "peanut gallery," "no can do," "grandfather clause," "low man on the totem pole," "hip hip hooray," and "Irish goodbye" are quite common in everyday communications; however, you may be surprised to learn that each has negative historical connotations. In addition, gender bias is quite common in our language. For instance, words like *mailman, salesman, policeman,* and *manpower* should be replaced with *mail carrier, salesperson, police officer,* and *workforce.* The following provides a few examples of biased language that could alienate your audience and reflect poorly on you as a presenter.

- *Gender* – congressman, businessman, man hours, man-made, man up, and female CEO are just a few examples. Note: remember that pronouns are no longer simply "he/him/his," "she/her/hers," or "they/them/theirs." Some presenters may choose to include their preferred pronouns in their introduction or on their opening slide. You could use your planning meetings to discuss the inclusion of pronouns, and ask the organization or person who hired you if there are any inclusion standards that you should honor.
- *Ability* – crippled, retarded, handicapped, lame, and spaz (among others). Note: we recommend using "person-first language" if you are referring to persons who are differently abled. So instead of "the autistic man," you could say "the person on the autism spectrum." Person-first language is recommended because it preserves the identity of the person themself, as opposed to labeling them by their disability. If you would like to read or learn more about how to speak about persons with disabilities, we recommend the work of Allison Hitt, a writing professor and disability advocate.
- *Sexual Orientation* – lezbo, homo, that's so gay, and tranny
- *Race and Ethnicity* – colored, bugger, gypped, hooligan, thug, nip, Oriental, towelhead, and welfare queen

Space Fillers

Excessive use of filler words (e.g., um, umkay?, right?, ah, like, so, and err) is a distraction to the audience, a reflection of anxiety, and a fluency diminisher. In fact, scholars call these filler words and phrases "filled pauses" (e.g., uh, um), "discourse markers" (e.g., I mean, you know, like), or "disfluencies."[38] Some studies have found that they can also lower the listener's perceptions of you as knowledgeable.[39] A space filler here or there (in our opinion, an average of 2–3 per minute), perhaps as a stumble or to indicate a moment for thinking, is not a significant issue. However, some scholars have found that "when filler words occur, the comprehension of the listener can be jeopardized or limited, causing the speaker to further lose credibility. The most effective speech occurs when filler words are used moderately."[40] In an effort to curb excessive fillers, researchers have shown that awareness training can improve this habit.[41]

Some presenters may be entirely unaware (see "Unconscious Incompetence" in Chapter 6) of the fact that they used 20 space fillers in the first 5–7 minutes—which diminishes credibility and clouds a speaker's message. If you pay close attention, you will notice that speakers often begin with a space filler: "Um, it's ah, good to be with you today" or "So, ah, it's good to be with you today!" Another common spot for space fillers is in between slides if an individual is using PowerPoint ("Um, the next slide shows…") or during the formal Q & A. In addition to single word space fillers, you may also notice speakers using filler phrases. These are phrases that are unknowingly over-used in the context of the talk. (e.g., "Does that make sense?," "and such," "you know what I mean?," "and everything like that," and "to be honest").

Completely eliminating space fillers is a difficult task, and takes practice. We find that practicing in advance and becoming more familiar with your material could increase your confidence and fluency with your talking points, and could cut down on space fillers. In addition, intentionally slowing down your pace of speech and pausing before you begin speaking or answering a question could give you a moment to think about how you want to begin your next point instead of starting with a space filler.

Delivering Bullet Points

When delivering a deck with a number of bullet points, *how* you navigate these slides can make all the difference. The reality is that the more text you have on a slide, the more likely it will force you to look at the slide or notes to read the text. This diminishes eye contact with the camera—which in our opinion, diminishes engagement. Our first recommendation for navigating slides with bullet points effectively is that when creating those slides, you want to minimize as much text as possible. Eliminate text that does not add to your message. Next, practice "capturing" a couple of bullets at once; Scott recommends that his students minimize the number of times they look at the list of bullet points to avoid the back and forth that often occurs when novice presenters navigate bullets. In other words, minimize the number of times you "look down/over." By doing so, you reduce the number of times you look away from the camera by 50 percent.

Mistake Recovery (Spoken)

> *"If you're not making mistakes then you're not doing anything. I'm positive that a doer makes mistakes."*
> —John Wooden, coach

It's not *if* you make a mistake, it's *when* you make a mistake. All presenters make mistakes. *Great* presenters take these in stride and do not make *more* of the mistake. Doing so only highlights your anxiety, your inadequacies, and/or the mistake itself (which many in the audience may miss). And emphasizing or backtracking to address a mistake only makes your audience feel uncomfortable.

When you make a mistake (e.g., choose the wrong word, provide the wrong statistic, temporarily lose your spot, forget a point you wanted to make, or say something before it appears on the slide), you have several options. First, you could "ask the audience" for help with the word or phrase you are stumbling on. This is a wonderful opportunity to get the word/phrase and then use self-deprecating humor and an opportunity for a laugh. In the past, Scott has made statements like, "Someone unmute and say the word I am trying to find!" Another option is the strategic pause with a sip of water while you buy some time and gather your thoughts. You can also ignore the mistake and restate the correct number or phrase: "I just said 32 seconds; I misspoke, it's 56. So, 56 seconds…". As previously mentioned, if you have good comedic timing, you can also make light of the miscue and get a laugh and proceed in a confident manner. One of Maria's strategies if she stumbles over a word while teaching is to make light of the time of day. If it's in the morning, she'll joke "Wow, I guess I need more coffee!" In the afternoon or early evening, she might say "Gosh, it's been a long day I guess!" Rarely is it appropriate to say "I'm sorry" or make a bigger deal of the misstep—drawing additional attention to it communicates nervousness, insecurity, or a lack of confidence.

As much as you will want it to be, your presentation will not be perfect (and that's ok!). For us, what is important is how you respond to the imperfection, and to do so with grace and humility. Watch the news or your favorite late-night show and pay close attention to how often the anchors or hosts make mistakes—to not only notice that they *do* happen, but also to see how they acknowledge (or simply move on from) the mistake. Do you even notice that a mistake was made? Most people do not, because those trained presenters are skilled at moving past them.

Unexpected Event Recovery

Similar to a verbal mistake, this is some other unplanned event that impacts your presentation. Be warned: an online presentation is ripe for miscues and unexpected problems, both in and out of your control. In recent months, we have experienced genuine tech issues, participant error, and presenter error, among other things. Similar to what we discussed in the previous section with "spoken mistake recovery," *how* you respond *when* these events occur, can make all the difference. If you let the audience know you are frazzled, or again, if you draw attention to the event, it will diminish your impact and may even make you look insecure, unprepared, or unprofessional. In all likelihood, you have seen and heard presenters who do not adapt well on the fly. While it can be stressful and upsetting when something unexpected interrupts your presentation, try to roll with the punches or make light of an unexpected event. *When* there's a problem, you can make a joke, buy time while the audio-visual gurus fix your problem, place the audience into a conversation to buy time, tell them what you *were* going to do, and so forth. Perhaps most important is to take a deep breath and if need be, go to contingency plans. Scott has finished the presentation via his iPhone and pulled out other laptops to make it work.

On the point of contingency plans, part of your pre-planning (which includes designing your space to try and ensure that your area is distraction-free and that your internet is working at its best capacity) should involve thinking about what you would do *if* and *when* something goes wrong (e.g., having your tablet or phone nearby with the appropriate online presentation app downloaded so you could log in there if something happens with your computer or your internet; having your slides downloaded as a file in a program that does not rely on the internet to work, like PowerPoint). Thinking about how you would respond *before* something happens will help you figure out how to respond *when* it happens.

Rambling

Rambling occurs for two primary reasons. In our experience, the first reason is that the presenter is not confident about their points. For example, in Tony Robbins' TED Talk, *Why We Do What We Do*, he rambles for the first four minutes and there does not seem to be a clear structure.[42] His slides contain different content than what he is discussing, he stops himself to make off-topic comments, and so forth. While viewing this clip, we were reminded of a statement made by Ed Markey, Vice President of Corporate Communications at Goodyear Tire & Rubber Co. He said that when it comes to online presentations in particular, "It takes another level of focus, to be sure you're staying on point." Brandon Charpied, Executive Director of the Management & Organizational Behavior Teaching Society, made a similar point and suggested that speakers must "stay concise, hit the highlights, allow for discussion, and keep everyone engaged and on their toes." These comments bring us to the second source of rambling: side comments that take the speaker off-topic or in a different direction. In this case, the speaker strays from their planned structure and begins discussing content that was not prepared. To be clear, extemporaneous remarks and discussion can be fine if the individual is disciplined, aware, and intentional about doing so. The problem with rambling is that speakers can easily lose their audience and may lose sight of their purpose and main message, and in some cases, become frustrated with you as a speaker. Indicators that a speaker is rambling include:

- switching topics in a variety of different directions without using oral signposts.
- using phrases like "which makes me think about," "this is off-topic, but...," "back on topic," "I digress," "as a side note," "that reminds me," or key words like "stray," "sidetrack," "deviate," "tangent," and "incidentally."
- spending a long time on one slide without referring to any of the content on it or advancing forward.

> *"I don't want to be boring. But that's not always easy."*
> —John Malkovich, actor

A theme we consistently heard from the executives we interviewed was the importance of a speaker's voice. A speaker's voice is his or her primary tool for engaging the audience. Karen Gilliam, Agency Chief Learning Officer & OD Capability Lead at NASA, reminded us of this reality when she suggested, "If you've got someone speaking in a monotone voice, it's just lulling you to sleep." Yes, it is—and one of our many purposes for writing this book is to help you avoid being that someone!

For an interesting take on this topic, take a look at Julian Treasure's TED Talk *How to Speak So That People Want to Listen*.[43] In fact, some research has found that a lively voice (i.e., vocal variety) is correlated with enthusiasm.[44] Other scholars have found that "varied delivery improves and listener comprehension."[45] Prosody is a set of speaking attributes that may include a speaker's pitch, loudness, pauses, intonation, and rhythm. These elements all contribute to the unique speaking style of each individual. For instance, the phrase "The ring was hers" is fairly benign from a semantic point of view. However, the phrase can take on a different meaning if it's spoken in certain ways.

Variations in volume, pitch, speed, or emphasis of keywords may change the meaning.[46]

The topic of voice can be further subdivided into a number of categories that warrant discussion. The keys to each of these topics are awareness and intentionality. As you read the following section, keep in mind the following piece of advice from Jennifer Cowles, Leader of Leadership and Executive Programs at KeyBank. She told us that "voice modulation is incredibly powerful in letting people know what you're passionate about, building on a particular point, or sharing *why* something is important."

The question to ask yourself is, "Am I aware of my default habits, and am I intentional when using, or not using, each?"

Rate of Speech/Speaking Pace – The intentional pacing of your talk is essential to its success. There is no concrete, agreed-upon range of speech, and ranges from different sources suggest anywhere from 120–225 words per minute.[47,48,49,50] For instance, according to one study, normal conversation lands in the range of 140–180 words per minute.[51] Another found that the delivery of a prepared script can exceed 200 words per minute.[52] For us, a good rule of thumb is the 120–220 range. Perhaps most important, your pace should speed up and slow down throughout your presentation, as opposed to remaining mechanically consistent throughout. The key is intentionality. Your speaking pace is a critical element for keeping your audience engaged and on the edge of their seats. It's also a critical ingredient for comprehension.[53] Many speakers do not intentionally pace themselves. Rather, most default to a pace that is often too fast or too slow. When the pace is too slow and accompanied by a monotone pitch, there is a high likelihood the speaker will be perceived as boring. If the pace is too fast, the speaker can be difficult to follow. Their sentences may run together or listeners may experience them as frazzled. Likewise, a fast pace can also communicate nerves or immaturity. A measured pace provides listeners with a break, an opportunity to follow along better, or (as we mentioned earlier), a moment to reflect on what was just said.

We are consistently amazed by how much better some speakers do when we coach them to slow down their pace. Their mind has more time to stay ahead and interestingly, other delivery challenges (e.g., jerkiness, space fillers, verbal mistakes, excessive movement) tend to diminish.

> *"If you want to connect, you must let them reflect."*
> —Darren Lacroix, speaker

Pauses/Silence – Pauses also have benefits for the speaker. When used effectively, pauses are powerful.[54] When reflecting on a presentation he gave for graduate school, Scott Taylor, Owner & Creative Director at BlkDog, told us that "in this unique setting, I had to slow down, pause intentionally, and recognize the areas where I could inject enthusiasm or emphasis, and adjust my tone to keep the audience's attention." Notice his statement about pausing intentionally. In fact, scholars have shown "that listeners were more likely to recognize words which had been encountered after silent pauses, demonstrating that silence affects not only the process of language comprehension but also its eventual outcome."[55] Pauses can communicate confidence and effective storytelling. They emphasize key points, and a well-placed pause helps the previous content "sink in." In addition, slight pauses have been shown to increase comprehension.[56,57] According to scholars, "Research observed that speech consists of short (0.15 s), medium (0.50 s), and long (1.50 s) pauses. Read speech tends to produce only short and medium pauses, while spontaneous speech shows more frequent use of medium and long pauses."[58] Of course, the pause can be overused and oddly placed, but in general, an intentional pause is an important tool in a speaker's ability to connect. And when you are giving online presentations, pauses could be especially important just in case a participant's sound cuts out momentarily; a pause on your end (even when you do not know that a participant's connection is poor) could allow their internet connection to catch up.

Volume/Loudness – Some speakers have a vocal volume that is too soft or too loud. Some studies have shown that volume or loudness is associated with perceived confidence.[59] Other scholars have associated the combination of rate of speech/speaking pace and volume/loudness (i.e., intensity) with perceived speaker confidence.[60] As with other aspects of vocal delivery, we suggest intentionality on the part of the speaker. If you are telling a story and want to add dramatic flair, lowering your voice and whispering can help your message connect. Or, if you are expressing frustration or anger, or simply emphasizing something of extreme importance, raising your voice can help as well.

Pitch – This refers to a speaker's frequency of sound. A speaker's intonation is a variation of pitch and can be experienced as high or low. Separate from the *natural* pitch of someone's voice, a speaker with a pitch that is constantly too high can come across to listeners as having a lack of confidence or authority. However, the high pitch may also communicate excitement (surely, you know someone whose voice gets higher...or louder...if they get excited). The key is an intentional pitch variation to communicate sentiment.[61,62] While it may not always be easy for every speaker to control the pitch of their voice, practicing within their natural pitch range can help them identify what works best. You do not want to *overexaggerate* by purposely raising your voice too high or lowering your voice; this will be evident (and sometimes off-putting) to an audience. Rather, try practicing with a variety of sentence types (imperative, declarative, exclamatory, or inquisitive). Does your voice go up at the end of a question? Is there more variation when you are exclaiming something with enthusiasm? How do you deliver an imperative command? Test all of these out to see how your voice sounds in different situations. Interestingly, one study found that "high speech rate and average pitch variation also resulted in higher ratings for male speakers."[63] This is less a commentary on the results of this one study and more about highlighting the importance of intentionally combining multiple elements such as smiling and variation in pitch, volume, and pace to yield necessary results.

Tone – The speaker's tone is used to express emotion or emphasize words or phrases. Tone can impact meaning or convey emotion. For example, "The speaker established a somber tone" would be delivered differently than "The speaker set an upbeat tone." Tone can be altered by modulating elements such as pitch, volume, pausing, and pace. It's important to ensure that as the speaker, you establish an emotional tone that aligns with your purpose/objectives. If the objective is to motivate and inspire, the tone may include elements such as an increased speaking pace, increased volume, and vocal variety to engage listeners. A somber tone will have a decreased pace, increased use of pauses, lower pitch, and potentially a lower volume.

Cadence/Rhythm – These terms refer to flow of words when speaking. For some, the flow is smooth and rhythmic. For other speakers, the flow can be experienced by listeners as abrupt, jerky, or uneven—components of a concept called speech disfluency, which "generally contains long pauses, discourse markers, repeated words, phrases or sentences and fillers or filled pauses like *uh* and *um*."[64] Another way of thinking of speech disfluency is when you think of someone whose presentation and speaking style could be characterized as "choppy." Speakers with abrupt pauses or phrasing can be distracting for listeners, which ultimately clouds their message.

Verbal Challenges

In addition to what we have mentioned above, there are a few other concepts we would like you to know about voice. What we discuss below are habits that may distract from your message. Again, a goal for you to work toward is reducing barriers that distract from placing your message center stage.

Chunking – At times, speakers combine words into a single chunked phrase, which makes it sound like one word or a continuous bombardment of content. This can occur when a speaker's pace is too quick or when English is not an individual's native language. Examples include "know-what-I-mean?", "what's-up-with-that?", or "whatcha-been-up-to?" In the southern United States, "all y'all's" often replaces "all of you." In a professional setting (and especially when you are presenting online where internet connections can vary), it's important that you let each word stand on its own and focus on slowing down.

Articulation – Articulation is the movement of the tongue, lips, jaw, and other organs to produce a sound. Articulation is important because it helps the audience better understand your message. Similar to chunking, inarticulate speech can occur when a speaker's pace is too quick or when English is not an individual's first language. Slowing down and carefully pronouncing words and phrases can help a speaker improve their articulation, which will then enhance the clarity and impact of what you are saying.

Vocal Fry and Upspeak – Readers familiar with any of the Kardashians have experienced this concept in action. In many ways, this concept is best learned through experience, so we encourage you to watch the video *Vocal Fry and Upspeak—Kate Kelleher*.[65] According to research, individuals experience these two in different ways. Some will experience vocal fry as annoying and may perceive the speaker as immature, unpleasant, lacking experience, and lacking authority.[66] Of course, there are cultural and gender differences, so there are no hard and fast rules. However, it's important to be aware of these verbal habits that *could* inhibit your ability to connect—especially with older audiences.[67]

Trailing Off – Trailing off (i.e., dropping phrases), means that the speaker's volume fades away at the end of a statement; if written out, there would be ellipses at the end of the sentence. Trailing off can communicate nerves, a lack of confidence, or a lack of experience. This habit most often occurs at the conclusion of a segment or worse, the end of the presentation, leading to awkward pauses where the audience doesn't know if they should applaud (virtually), if it's time to shift into Q & A, or if they can sign off. In short, trailing off at the end is not the best way to finish strong. To avoid trailing off, pay close attention to your conclusion and ensure that your volume and pitch stay consistent through your final sentence. In our experience, trailing off is often associated with poor eye contact with the camera, which is a terrible final impression. Keep the volume, pitch, and eye contact consistent and finish strong. You could even add in a smile, a nod, and a "thank you" to clearly signal the end.

Delivery/Nonverbal

Intentional Movement

While seated presenters cannot use their online space in the same way as they would live, there still is an opportunity to use intentional movement as a way to emphasize, underscore, or assist in making a point. Perhaps the presenter moves toward the camera, or leans back to reflect or communicate a pensive moment. Movement remains useful in an online environment, but it's critical that the movement is controlled, intentional, and *adds to the delivery*.

Hand Gestures

According to scholars, hand gestures when communicating transcend cultural and linguistic boundaries.[68] And while we know they are important to speech and communication, there are competing theories as to *why*.[69] Regardless of *why*, research suggests that gestures "can alter the interpretation of speech, disambiguate speech, increase comprehension and memory, and convey information not delivered by speech."[70] Similar to what we said about movement in the previous section, it is crucial that a presenter's use of hands is both intentional and balanced. In fact, "being able to see the face and hand movements of a speaker facilitates language comprehension."[71] Although it can be difficult to incorporate hand gestures into an online presentation, any hand gestures you do use in an online setting should accentuate your main points, add to the story, and be regarded as another tool to help engage listeners. In the context of online presentations, hands normally rest comfortably on the tabletop, and depending on your distance from the camera, gestures look most natural when kept near the top of your sternum.

Toastmasters explicitly highlights three types of hand gestures: conventional, emotional, and descriptive. According to its manual *Using Body Language*:

- "Conventional gestures are symbols for words, such as the raised hand for the word 'stop' and two raised fingers for the number two.

- Descriptive gestures describe the idea you are communicating, such as holding the hands apart to show length or moving the hands and arms to indicate shape.
- Emotional gestures suggest feelings, such as shaking a clenched fist to show anger or determination or shrugging the shoulders to show indifference."[72]

There have been a few common mistakes that we consistently see when watching online presentations. In these instances, the presenter:

- unknowingly plays with their fingers.
- fails to keep their gestures close to their chest and as a result, their gestures look as though they are going to hit the camera.
- has overly stiff/straight fingers, which looks awkward.
- fails to use gestures and misses an opportunity to emphasize key points.
- uses gestures that are jerky, bouncy, or abrupt.

What's most important is that you identify a process that looks natural and communicates professionalism. According to Van Edwards, "The bottom TED Talks had an average of 124,000 views and used an average of 272 hand gestures during the 18-minute Talk. The top TED Talks had an average of 7,360,000 views and used an average of 465 hand gestures—that's almost double!"[73] This suggests some degree of connection between the use of hand gestures and an appealing presentation. And while TED Talks are "in-person" presentations, we nonetheless assert that hand gestures are just as relevant to online communication.

Fluent Transitions

While not a make-or-break element of presentation skills, we do believe fluent transitions are important because transitioning between slides well or switching between Zoom screens can make you look really polished. In our experience, when moving between slides (or Zoom screens), most people pause, look at the screen, reach for their mouse or lean forward to advance the slide, let out a big space filler, and then continue on. As a result, there is an odd and abrupt pause in the flow of the presentation. You will look more polished if, as you are saying the last few words on a slide, you advance to the next, while saying, "another interesting statistic we discovered was…" or something similar. For your audience, you didn't miss a beat—and not only will this approach increase the fluency of your presentation, *but you will also* engage the audience for longer periods of time.

Eye Contact

When presenting online, eye contact will most likely be the largest shift. One theme that we consistently heard from our interviewees was how awkward it feels for students and clients making the transition to be looking at people on a computer screen, not at their faces in person. In fact, Aaron Beverly, 2019 Toastmasters World Champion of Public Speaking, told us, "The biggest adjustment that I had to make is honestly looking at the camera lens. That was really a struggle for me…sometimes I will look slightly off-camera to relieve participants of the eye contact."

Let's take a moment to highlight that. Eye contact in this medium means that you look directly into the lens of your camera—NOT at the computer screen. Remember the following phrase as you practice: **Eye to Eye**. *In other words, your eyes on the eye of the camera.*

Not only does looking into the camera feel awkward at first (because it technically means that you are not looking at the screen or the faces of any of the participants), but the amount of time you are required to do so can feel unnatural as well. Most presenters want to look at their other monitor, to the faces of participants online, or down at their notes or script.

The challenge with these approaches is that they are the equivalent of looking away from your audience in a live presentation. And everyone reading this book understands what it feels like when presenters look at the screen or down at the ground—it communicates nerves, a lack of confidence, a lack of preparation, and at times, a lack of experience presenting online.

There are a few common mistakes that we consistently observe when watching online presentations. In these instances, the presenter:

- has not placed their camera at eye level.
- has placed their camera at an odd angle.
- has not checked how their glasses impact eye contact with their audience.
- looks down, up, or to the side for long periods of time.
- reads the entire presentation, which means that their eyes are looking at the screen and moving methodically from left to right.

Eye contact is critical. It's the glue that keeps people engaged. By engaging the audience through eye contact, you have the opportunity to connect, build rapport, and involve participants. Maintain steady eye contact with the camera (at least 80% of the time).

Facial Expressions

Facial expressions complement your spoken words, hand gestures, and eye contact. Your facial expressions also communicate emotion (e.g., anxiety, happiness, fear, disgust) and we assert that facial expressions can communicate confidence and skill in your craft. And in an online environment where your natural movements and connection with the audience are limited, your facial expressions are crucial for enhancing messages that you want to send to your audience. The critical element is a concept called congruence. Congruence means that your verbals and nonverbals are aligned. A classic example of incongruence is when a speaker says, "I am so excited to be here" but their nonverbals and voice communicate an entirely different message (as in, our facial expression is blank or bored, we are sitting or slouching without much engagement, and our voices are monotonous). When a person is authentically excited, their eyes get bigger, and they deliver a Duchenne smile. When people are "concerned," nonverbals may include narrowing the eyes, a look off to the side, and closing the mouth. These nonverbals are often aligned with a slower pace, a lower volume, and long pauses for effect. To be truly impactful, your facial expressions must be congruent with your spoken message. This is especially important online because your face is right there on everyone's screen and is visible to every participant (as opposed to those who sit in the back of the auditorium and can't see your face clearly when you're on the stage in person).

Think about your favorite actor for a moment. Let's say everything in their performance is aligned—voice, eyes, hand gestures, the lines—except their facial expressions lack congruence with the requirements of the script. They would lose their job. Think of the nonverbal elements that we've described as an important part of your "act," and an essential element of your on-screen "character."

Nonverbals to Avoid

When combined, the nonverbals highlighted in this section work together to aid in your delivery of a successful online performance. Solid eye contact, appropriate hand gestures, smooth transitions, and congruent facial expressions each help you tell the story. We have noticed a few nonverbal behaviors that we would encourage you to minimize or avoid.

Lack of Preparation/Appearing Befuddled – The presenter has a "deer in headlights" moment as if the presentation they are about to give is a big surprise. The speaker nonverbally communicates that they are disorganized, past their prime, confused, or mystified by the entire experience. Not only does this reflect poorly on the presenter, but this behavior also reflects poorly on the organization hosting the event. As we mentioned before, saying "I am still learning how to use this technology" is no longer acceptable, nor is it an excuse.

Slouching – The speaker is hunched and unaware of their posture for much of the presentation. Slouching is often associated with "looking to the side" and can communicate a lack of interest, energy, and professionalism, and when combined with a monotone voice and a slow pace, it yields an uninspiring spectacle.

Bouncing/Rocking/Swaying – The speaker is moving unintentionally. We have seen many variations of this. In some instances, the speaker rocks back and forth, which appears as moving away from the camera and then into the camera. Maria participated in an online session where the presenter rocked back and forth during the entire session (and had the computer on their lap), and it was somewhat unnerving to watch the presenter be constantly in motion—moving toward the camera and getting larger, and then moving backward—while speaking. In other instances, the speaker bounces or swivels without awareness of their distracting behaviors.

Scratching/Touching Face – The speaker itches or touches their face or head too much (like constantly playing with their hair). A few instances of this will unlikely be noticed, but some presenters struggle to control this nonverbal behavior and it can communicate nerves, anxiety, or poor hygiene.

Conclusion—You Shine Through

Based on our experience, the content of Chapter 5 can be the most difficult piece of the equation. It takes a great deal of practice, feedback, and experience to master the many dimensions of delivery. The good news is that we believe that anyone with the motivation, time, and coaching can improve their delivery and connect with their audience. It's the last piece of the puzzle. Your personality shines through in a way that connects with your audience. You have the message, the visuals, and the delivery. Aligning these three major ingredients may seem herculean at first, but after time, it becomes habit...a way of being.

So how do you get to a place where you can "just turn it on?" Like anything else, there are very few shortcuts. However, we have identified a few critical suggestions that will accelerate your growth. Continual growth is the topic of Chapter 6. In that chapter, we explore the four stages of competence, deliberate practice, and Captovation, which is an AI-powered technology designed to provide you with analytics and data. We also help you begin to think about prioritization. At first, it can feel overwhelming, so we conducted an informal survey via social media platforms to identify some potential starting points.

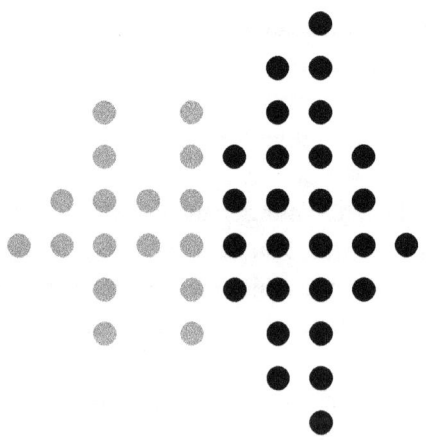

CHAPTER 6:
DESIGN FOR CONTINUAL GROWTH

"Picture your brain forming new connections as you meet the challenge and learn. Keep on going."

—Carol Dweck, *Mindset*

For many of you, presenting online is still a relatively new medium, and one that you may not like, nor were you trained in school (or maybe even early in your careers) to present online. As a result, the sudden shift can feel uncomfortable and awkward at first. There are a few pieces of good news, though. First, people are generally patient and understanding as we all learn this new medium. While this patience will not last forever, it does buy you time to master this domain. The second piece of good news is that when you do master online presentations, you will stand out from the crowd. You can quickly gain visibility and display mastery if you approach learning in a certain way. This chapter is designed to provide you with some critical information that will help you master the domain more quickly and captivate those who attend your presentations.

Many of the tried and tested interventions still hold true.

To improve, you can:

- secure a presentation skills coach.
- recruit an ally who will provide you with feedback.
- record your online presentations and perform the analytics.
- conduct a practice session with colleagues.
- take a course via Dale Carnegie or others.
- join a group such as Toastmasters.
- listen to podcasts on the topic of presentation skills.

However, there are other tools that may in fact accelerate your growth and development. For instance, the Captovation Platform (www.captovation.ai) provides you with concrete analytics on any number of dimensions of your presentations (e.g., pace, space fillers, keywords). In addition to the analytics, Captovation provides developmental feedback and tutorials to help you improve and grow.

Today, we turn to technology to track everything from athletic performance to personal goals to productivity. Presentation skills and communication are no different. And while technology is an important tool, there are some critical elements that will accelerate your growth if you internalize and act upon them. The following sections are designed to do so.

Understanding Growth—The Four States of Competence

The four states of competence model is the work of Noel Burch. Originally called *The Four Stages of Learning Any New Skill*, Burch designed the model in the 1970s.[74] According to the model, there are four states of competence and when you think about any skill you have ever learned, like driving, the piano, a video game, or public speaking, his work has a lot of face validity. In other words, it just makes sense. The dimensions of this model include the following:

1. *Unconscious Incompetence (UI).* Unconscious Incompetence means that you do not know what you do not know. From a presentation perspective, this is a speaker who uses too many space fillers or vocal fry and has never even been exposed to these concepts. For those of you who learned about technology in Chapter 4, it's likely you had never heard of a "ring light" or a "soft box"; in other words, you were blissfully in a UI space.
2. *Conscious Incompetence (CI).* Conscious Incompetence means that the learner is acutely aware of how far they have to go before displaying mastery. Returning to Chapter 4 about technology, some of our interviewees told us that they felt a little overwhelmed by all they need to know about technology. In the context of speaking online, CI occurs after an individual has learned the concepts of vocal fry or upspeak and then "sees" themselves using those concepts during a video analysis session with a coach. The individual knows the concepts and is aware of the gap between their current skills and a desired future state.
3. *Conscious Competence (CC).* Conscious Competence means that if our fictitious online presenter engages in deliberate practice and concentrates really hard, they can begin to minimize the number of space fillers, vocal fry, and upspeak. However, it takes a lot of concentration and is not yet at a place of automaticity. CC requires feedback—from a coach or a peer.
4. *Unconscious Competence (UC).* Unconscious Competence happens after significant practice—oftentimes with the guidance of a coach or mentor. At this point, our example presenter has worked hard to eliminate vocal fry, upspeak, and space fillers over a period of time

and no longer needs to think about any of these concepts. The area of development has been fixed or occurs rarely. And while the speaker has progressed in these three areas, they are likely at a place of unconscious incompetence on other, more advanced topics like comedic timing, or advanced storytelling.

Each of you reading this book, and we as authors, are moving along the states of competence on any number of different topics—just within this one domain of online presentations! So be patient, prioritize your areas of improvement, and engage in deliberate practice to help expedite the process.

Deliberate Practice

"With deliberate practice, however, the goal is not just to reach your potential but to build it, to make things possible that were not possible before. This requires challenging homeostasis—getting out of your comfort zone—and forcing your brain or your body to adapt."

—K. Anders Ericsson, *Peak: Secrets from the New Science of Expertise*

Scholar K. Anders Ericsson was an expert on how people become experts. While there are a number of elements embedded in his work (see the book *Peak: Secrets from the New Science of Expertise* for an incredible read on how people build skill), they can be simplified to include four primary elements: time, repetition, real-time coaching/feedback, and working on skills outside of your current abilities.[75] If you want to develop yourself to become a world-class cello player, surgeon, or pilot, the recipe for success involves time, repetition, real-time coaching and feedback from a mentor, and working on skills outside of your current ability level.

We would assert that presenting online is no different. However, when it comes to public speaking, we find that hierarchy, politics, and power dynamics cloud the process in organizational life. For instance, think of a senior leader in your organization who wants to improve their presentation skills. After their horribly exhausting and poorly-delivered talk, they call and ask, "How did that go?" If you are like most people, you respond with "Great! It was good!" and you leave it there.

The reality is that senior leaders rarely receive unfiltered and honest feedback about how they performed. There is often an element of fear among subordinates, so they are cloistered from honest, unfiltered feedback. While they may improve over time, the rate of improvement could occur so much more quickly and many of their foibles will remain in the realm of Unconscious Incompetence.

> *"There are always three speeches, for every one you actually gave. The one you practiced, the one you gave, and the one you wish you gave."*
>
> —Dale Carnegie, *How to Win Friends and Influence People*

So here are some critical questions. Who is your ally or coach in your organization? Do you have an external coach? Who will provide you with unfiltered and authentic feedback? Are you perceived as someone who is open to feedback? Are you seeking it out? Every time you speak, is there something you are actively practicing and focusing on for improvement (e.g., storytelling, limiting space fillers)? If so, is someone in the audience paying close attention to your every move so they can provide feedback? Reflection on each of these questions is critical. If you want to progress through all four states of competence, you need to engage in deliberate practice—it's as simple as that. We are confident that a lack of deliberate practice is the root of the problem—the real reason we spend an inordinate amount of time sitting through poorly designed, poorly delivered online presentations. Now, think about the damage these presentations do to employee engagement and motivation and the billions of dollars in wasted time each year. It's astonishing, but each of us can be a part of the solution.

Quantify Growth/Seek Data

Even when you do have a coach or colleague who is open and honest with you, it can be helpful to have quantifiable data. Fortunately, Microsoft Teams and other online platforms make it easy for you to capture the video *and* audio so you can conduct the analysis—either by hand or with the help of technology (visit www.captovation.ai). Captovation (the software platform) is designed to quantify many dimensions of your presentation. In addition to providing a transcript of your talk, the AI-powered system tracks the following:

- a self-reported score of confidence and anxiety
- the title of the presentation and desired length
- the actual length of presentation
- words per minute, or pace of speaking (WPM)
- space fillers used per minute (SFPM)
- words that communicate emotion—sentiment analysis
- words/phrases that communicate a lack of inclusivity
- words that communicate gratitude
- words that communicate business savviness
- words that communicate research/preparation
- oral signposts that indicate a sound presentation structure
- specific, predetermined words that the user would like to track

Some have said that "data is the new gold," and while we are using the statement slightly out of the context for which it was intended, we believe that the more data you have, the better. For instance, if you tell us that an educator for a 50-minute class had a slow pace, a monotonous pitch, used zero words that communicate enthusiasm, said four space fillers per minute, and went over the expected time by five minutes, we would place a bet on the student experience of that online course—not good.

In addition to individual use cases, when possible, use technology like *Captovation* to quantify growth over time. For instance, if data across three presentations suggests that the educator we mentioned moved their pace into acceptable boundaries, varied their pitch, reduced their space fillers to only two per minute, used ten words that communicate enthusiasm, and finished on time, we would place a different bet on the student experience. Of course, it's not a sure thing, but the data would suggest a better learning experience.

Self-Awareness & Feedback

Embedded in this entire process of learning and growing is the concept of self-awareness. We assert that the more *aware* you are as a presenter, the better you will *be* as a presenter. For each of us to become more self-aware, we have to seek out and be open to feedback. While technology is a critical part of that equation, the human element is just as important. The technology cannot 100% diagnose the two cases at the end of the previous section. The data, *along with* human interpretation, make a powerful combination.

Perhaps the most important piece of information we can provide is the crucial nature of this topic. Feedback will fuel your progress. If you are open and seeking it out, you will thrive. If you are closed and afraid of it, you will miss an important opportunity to shine.

Prioritization

When we are coaching students or clients and they move from Unconscious Incompetence to Conscious Incompetence, we often see a look of horror fall upon their faces as they process *all* that needs to be improved.

Part of our work is to take the data and establish the path forward. Like an educator does when they are planning each week and even each day of their courses, the work needs to be scaffolded in a way where a combination of simple skills leads to more complex skills. For instance, we have used the term "vocal variety," which is a combination of many different elements of voice. However, in presenting feedback and coaching to a student or client, we would not start by simply saying "you need to improve your vocal variety," because that may be too overwhelming and too complex to comprehend. Instead, we may first challenge our clients to intentionally work on their pacing, and once that's under control, then we may work on volume or pitch.

To help you get a sense of what matters most to audiences when they are watching online presentations, we conducted an informal Google Form poll that we shared via social media platforms. We obtained the responses of 100 business professionals about the importance of several dimensions of online presentations, which are organized in Table 1. We asked about technology, aspects of nonverbal communication, delivery, structure, and so forth. Before we share the results, it's critical to underscore the importance of context (or all of the elements surrounding the situation—people, platform, purpose, time of day, level of formality, topic, etc.). *Your* context (e.g., school, organization, association) may value some of these elements over others, so it's important to discuss this list with mentors or your supervisor. We also want to note that ours was a survey conducted via social media and is not intended to be rigorous scientific research. It's simply a snapshot of what 100 executives think and feel about online presentations.

To set the stage, we asked participants to rate each item on a 7-point scale with two anchors: 1 (Not Very Important) and 7 (Very Important). The results are divided by topic and placed in order of importance.

Table 1
What Is Most Important to 100 Leaders?

The Presenter's Technology

The presenter's sound is crisp and clear.	6.73
The presenter's internet speed is adequate.	6.55
The presenter's technology functions well.	6.52
The presenter's setting/background is engaging, not distracting.	5.66
The presenter is well-lit.	5.35
The presenter's camera angle (straight on/eye-to-eye level).	5.20

The Presenter's Structure

The presenter's purpose/objectives are clear.	6.27
The presenter's agenda/roadmap is clear.	6.08
The presenter's introduction is engaging.	5.89
The presenter's thesis and supporting materials are clear.	5.79
The presenter's conclusion is powerful.	5.77
The presenter recaps what's been covered.	5.59
The presenter's explained norms for the session.	5.30
The presenter sends materials prior to the meeting/workshop.	4.40

The Presenter's Delivery

The presenter is competent with using the platform (e.g., Zoom, Teams).	6.35
The presenter is enthusiastic and excited to share their content.	6.29
The presenter's slides are easily understood/intuitive.	6.11
The presenter adheres to established time boundaries.	6.09
The presenter sets a conversational, yet professional tone.	5.90
The presenter's slides do not have excessive text or complicated graphics.	5.85
The presenter speaks extemporaneously and does not read their presentation.	5.79
The presenter uses vocal variation effectively (e.g., tone, pitch, pace, volume).	5.66
The presenter is skilled at "bringing the audience along".	5.59
The presenter uses words that breathe life and color into the presentation.	5.51
The presenter avoids excessive use of space fillers (e.g., um, ah, eh, er, so).	5.31
The presenter makes eye contact with the camera.	4.97
The presenter is dressed appropriately.	4.78
The presenter uses hand gestures effectively.	4.46
The presenter incorporates multiple tools (e.g., chat, polls, video, breakouts).	4.25

The informal poll results reveal that tech basics are important to respondents. Internet connectivity and crisp sound are highly valued as a starting point (and as you will recall, a microphone or quality headset will be important considerations in helping your audience members hear and see you clearly from the beginning of your presentation). When it comes to structure, a clear purpose, roadmap, and strong introduction were most valued—which suggests that your audience will feel informed and comfortable when they know what you are presenting about, and how your time together will be organized. From a delivery standpoint, respondents value presenters who know the technology, are enthusiastic about their content, and present slides that are easily understandable.

We aim for the results of our informal survey to provide you with general guidance as you think about where to begin. Most importantly, we recommend that you only select one or two items for practice at a time. Do not try to fix everything at once—that's setting yourself up for frustration and failure. Pick one element, bring that skill or item to a place of unconscious competence, and then move on to the next.

> *"This is hard. This is fun."*
> —Carol Dweck, *Mindset*

Conclusion—Hard & Fun

We really enjoy the work of Carol Dweck. She beautifully captures the mindset needed to succeed at mastering presentation skills. The process can be tiresome, frustrating, and challenging, but after time, it can become enjoyable and a *good* kind of challenge. We began the book by discussing Dweck's concept of a growth mindset as a way of being that will accelerate and promote your growth. The good news is that our move to online presentations has actually accelerated the ability for technology to augment our growth with analytics and data. This data, in the hands of a human coach, is the equivalent of a physician with the results of your complete blood count (CBC). A trained expert with the data can more quickly identify a path forward.

These six chapters have examined and provided you with *a lot* of information about how to become a good online presenter, when you are in the spotlight role. With that focus, we have talked a lot about how your choices impact the audience, and how you can make good, well-informed decisions that will keep *your* audience members engaged and responsive. And if this is what you want out of your audience members, we hope that you would want to return the same responsiveness and involvement to the presenters whose sessions *you* observe. So in Chapter 7, we explore the flip side—your role and responsibilities as a participant. The reality is that we are all participants some of the time. And even in that (sometimes) more passive role, your *brand* is still on display. We want you to remember in those moments that participation requires design as well—whether the presentation is a webinar or a meeting, whether you will be on video or only on audio, and even whether you're interested in the topic or not. When you think about your "typical behaviors" as a participant in online presentations or meetings, ask yourself this (and answer honestly): *is my participation style "on brand," or does it need some work?*

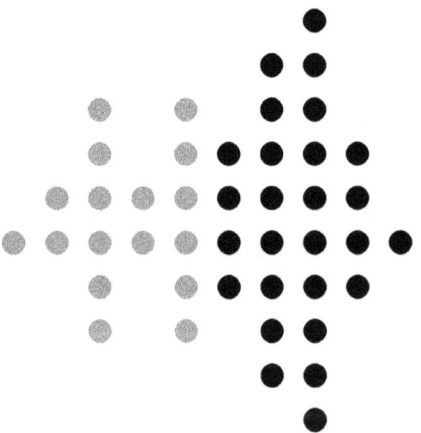

CHAPTER 7:
DESIGN YOUR PARTICIPATION

"When present, be present."

—Brian Fishel,
Chief Human Resources Officer, KeyBank

While this book focuses on the role of a presenter in an online presentation, we would do our readers a disservice if we did not cover the topic of how to be a prepared and engaged participant. As you read this chapter, reflect on your participation in any webinars, meetings, or online sessions you have tuned in for and sat through, and ask yourself: what message were you communicating? *The Boston Globe* published an article titled *The 12 Most Annoying Co-Workers You Face on Zoom*,[76] and we have included a sample below. We're sure that these will provide you with a laugh, perhaps because they may remind you of someone you work with—and even we can identify people we work with who illustrate these superlatives:

- The "I Couldn't Be Bothered to Pick Up"
- The Tech-Challenged
- The Poor Internet Connection
- The Proud Parent
- The Multi-Tasker
- The Hijacker
- The "I Thought This Was a Lunch Meeting"
- The Invisible Co-Worker
- The Extroverted Thinker

We are sure that many of you reading are acutely aware of proper etiquette when "live," but online, new norms are forming, and we believe that they deserve consideration. In addition to the participant Google Form poll that we shared in Chapter 6, we conducted a second informal poll that was also shared via social media platforms to obtain the feedback of 41 managers about online meeting participant behaviors. The results are organized in Table 2 below. Similar to the previous survey, it was conducted via social media and is not intended to be rigorous scientific research. It's simply a snapshot of what 41 managers think and feel about online participation. We asked participants to rate each item on a 7-point scale with two anchors: 1 (Not Very Important) and 7 (Very Important). The results are placed in order of importance.

Table 2
What Is Most Important When Participating Online?

The participant's sound is crisp and clear.	6.27
The participant's technology functions well.	6.12
The participant is competent with the meeting platform (e.g., Zoom, Skype, Teams).	5.97
The participant's internet speed is adequate.	5.90
The participant is not multitasking (e.g., doing other work, texting).	5.73
The participant is asking questions verbally or in the chat feature when appropriate.	5.65
The participant displays nonverbals that communicate engagement (e.g., nodding, eye contact).	5.19
The participant's camera angle is suitable for seeing their whole face at an eye-to-eye level.	5.00
The participant is well-lit.	4.90
The participant's setting/background is professional.	4.75
The participant has their video turned on during the meeting.	4.65
The participant's pets/children are not consistently on screen.	4.63
The participant is dressed professionally (for your organization).	4.48

Similar to the poll in Chapter 6, managers value employees with clear sound, high-functioning technology, and fast internet speed. It will also be important to minimize multitasking and display engagement by asking questions. On one note, while our poll did not yield similar results, a theme among the managers we spoke with was placing high value on team members who choose to be on camera and are engaged. To be clear, we are not saying here that from our standpoint, it is a requirement for you to be on camera; we understand that "video on" is a complicated topic, and that is best left up to managers and supervisors to decide. We simply *recommend* that you turn your video on if you are comfortable and able to do so, because it will enhance your professional image.

Ultimately, the primary topic underpinning this chapter is impression management. A simple way to think about impression management is that it's the process by which you intentionally design how others perceive you. Most often, it is choosing to behave in ways that will cause others to think highly of you. In live presentations, it should be generally understood that playing on your phone, acting disinterested, engaging in side conversations, and showing up late are behaviors that will not serve you well—especially when those specific behaviors are not widely accepted.

So, then, how do you cause others to think highly of you when you are a participant in an online environment? First of all, be aware of the fact that if your face is visible on the video of an online presentation, *the presenter will be paying attention to what you are reflecting back to them.* We recently spoke with a senior leader in a Fortune 500 corporation who said that they would often scan the audience to see who looks engaged, and who looks "checked out." Effective teachers do this as well; you can tell when someone is confused, interested, hostile, or even might have a question based on their body language and facial expressions. So if you "read the screen" and study the audience while you are presenting, you may be able to change your approach, pause for a moment and ask for questions, or take a step back to clarify.

This chapter will explore some new norms, and help you design how you show up. We believe that being a good participant represents an opportunity to accelerate your career. Similarly, we also think online behavior has the potential to stall careers. A good rule of thumb is to follow the lead of your supervisor—if they are on screen, you should be on screen as well. If they are in business casual dress, you should match their level of dress. While these are not hard and fast rules, it's a starting place. What follows is a list of considerations so that you can present your best self.

Setting & Background

As we discussed, your background is the new first impression. And while the first context of that comment was about your setting and background as the presenter, we believe that you should be just as conscious of these elements as a participant. The reality is that people's homes and apartments communicate a message. They form an impression. If you are on camera and "letting a presenter into your work-at-home world," what is the impact you would like to make? Does your background communicate that you are a high-potential business professional, or do you look like you are in a college dormitory or childhood bedroom? Our purpose is not to belittle childhood bedrooms or sparsely decorated apartments. The more significant point is that you think critically about the impression you want to give, and then design a setting that aligns with your objectives—to the best of your ability, of course, since we understand that there may be limitations in your work-at-home environment.

If you are using the "add a background" feature, purchase one of the green screens we mentioned earlier in the book to help you look much more professional, not like a ghostly figure moving in and out of focus. Like the comment above, choose a background image that aligns with the impression you want to make on others. If you wish to effuse a "company person" impression, maybe you share a corporate image that has meaning to your organization. On the other hand, if you want to set a more light-hearted and playful tone, it could be a more playful image. Or, it could be something simple like a plain-colored background that helps you stand out more visibly (remember, don't choose a green background if you're wearing green that day!).

If you choose not to upload a virtual background and remain off video, be aware of the impression this conveys to authority figures. Some may consider this behavior a "red flag." Remaining off-screen can communicate disengagement, disinterest, distraction, poor hygiene, or a lack of preparation. It's essential that you pay close attention to the implicit and explicit norms in your context, and remember that everything you do conveys a message.

Behaviors to avoid:

- slouching on your couch
- crouching in a closet
- visible mess or clutter
- to the extent possible, being in a space where there is a lot of commotion and noise (even if you are muted for the majority of the session, what happens when you are called on to speak, or have an important question?)
- inappropriate or distracting backgrounds (e.g., video of palm trees blowing in the wind)

Technology

Chapter 4 covers this topic in great depth, and we would encourage you to review our suggestions because the content is just as relevant for participants as it is for presenters. We have colleagues who, even four months into a more virtual environment, still show up confused, unprepared, and have done little to address their poor internet connections, lack of lighting, and cavernous sound. Every time they speak in a meeting, people need to say, "Alice, you are on mute," and when they do unmute, their contribution has a metallic and broken sound.

Ensure that your technological needs are met. If finances are a concern, speak with your supervisor about support to ensure that you have the internet speed, equipment, lighting, sound quality, and cameras to ensure success. By doing so, you will limit distractions and ensure that your participation, from a technology perspective, is professional, polished, and running smoothly.

Behaviors to avoid:

- telling everyone how old your computer is
- complaining to everyone how slow your internet is
- stating that you don't know the technology, like an apology or caveat
- lighting only half of your face
- forgetting to place yourself on mute—especially if you own a dog, have a baby, or have angry teenagers in your home

Participation

> *"You are paid to have an opinion; therefore, speak up and add to the discussion."*
> —Brian Fishel, Chief Human Resources Officer, KeyBank

One way to show engagement is to actively participate in the discussion or dialogue. Even a quick statement like "I agree with Sharmaine" can send the message that you are engaged and involved. Of course, asking an insightful question of the presenter, contributing to polls, or being actively involved in breakout rooms each communicates engagement.

Be mindful, too, that recorded presentations may also generate a file of what is discussed in the chat box (like Zoom)—and that includes private messages sent from one user to another. So as Maria has stated in her syllabus, *do not write something in the chat, in a private message to someone else, that you would not want everyone to read.*

Behaviors to avoid:

- over-participating
- turning off your camera if the norm is for it to be on (unless there is a reason that you have perhaps communicated to your supervisor in advance)
- being overly negative and complaining about "The New Normal"
- if applicable, attending an entire meeting without your presence being known—in the chat, via a spoken comment, asking a question, etc.
- holding a visual aid too close to the camera (it gets too big for viewers)
- personal conversations in the chat feature

Nonverbal Behaviors

Nonverbals that communicate engagement online are somewhat nuanced and largely depend on your specific context. However, we feel strongly that there are some hallmarks to consider—especially because these cues are crucial for the presenter, who will be looking to audience members for reactions, engagement, and all forms of feedback throughout the presentation. So when your video is on, are you nodding your head when people make comments that you agree with? In a similar vein, are you smiling when someone makes a joke? Or do you continue to stoically stare off to the side like you did not hear anything? If you have never presented online before, we want you to know—as teachers and presenters—that it is difficult to get a sense of audience engagement just from looking at the computer screen, so your attentiveness is even more critical in the online environment. One of the most challenging aspects of shifting to online teaching when the pandemic first struck was getting a sense of whether or not students were actually interested and engaged. Everyone's facial expressions look the same when they're all staring at the computer screen...and unlike a classroom, or an in-person presentation environment, you do not know what they are looking at. Seeing someone laugh (on mute) at an inappropriate time, for example, could cause the presenter to become unnerved. We say this not only to emphasize the importance of your active and engaged presence, but to show that the way you act when you are on camera as a participant is equally important to help the presenter be successful.

Participant eye contact online is a little more nuanced, because people's eyes will be looking at their screens; similar to what we discussed above with nonverbal behaviors, it's easiest to tell if they are paying attention by their reactions to comments made by the presenter.

Behaviors to avoid:

- allowing your pets to move across the screen/holding your cat
- reading something (an article, a text/email, etc.) that is going to provoke emotional reactions (disgust, laughter, etc.) that would be inappropriate for the session
- appearing in a way on camera that is inconsistent with what your coworkers would see from you in the office environment, even on "casual Friday"
- consistently looking off in the distance, as if you're watching TV or talking to someone else in your workspace

Dress & Hygiene

Dress truly depends on the norms in your context. It's best to match your immediate supervisor and while they may not explicitly state the preferred norm, you can readily gauge the appropriate attire by closely observing your supervisor or their supervisor.

Similarly, basic hygiene is another way to communicate that you are prepared and have put some forethought into the meeting. We have seen colleagues in a number of contexts who *never* would have "shown up" the way they have online—who never would have "shown up" the way they have online—underdressed, unshaven, and looking disheveled or like they just finished a workout or got out of bed five minutes before the session. While it's not necessarily expected that you wear *exactly* what you would wear to the office for every meeting, we suggest that your general appearance communicates your interest in and dedication to the session (attendance at which may be a required part of your job responsibilities).

Conclusion—When Present, Be Present

It's quite simple: How you show up as a participant either adds to or detracts from your brand. For each of you reading this text, that equation will look a little different. In some contexts, the decision-makers value you being on screen, dressed professionally, and actively participating. In other contexts, the person presenting isn't even on screen themselves (or, in a Zoom webinar, for instance, "video on" isn't even an option). What's critical is that you have the social awareness to understand the norms in your context. A good rule of thumb is to be just a step above or in alignment with authority figures. By doing so, you align yourself with decision makers and position yourself in a positive light, showing that you are ready to listen, learn, and participate.

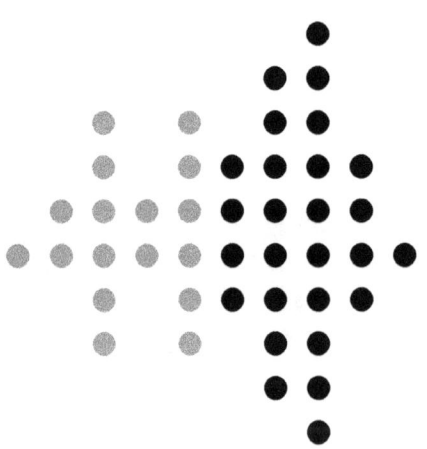

CONCLUSION

"Your ability to communicate with others will account for fully 85% of your success in your business and in your life."

—Brian Tracy, author

Two words have implicitly and explicitly formed threads that are woven throughout the narrative of this book: intentionality and design. We believe that there is great power in combining them as you think about every aspect of your work as a presenter. After you have finished your design work (and still with plenty of time before your presentation), step back and take inventory as you enter the revision stage (which is Maria's favorite because when it comes to writing in particular, she believes that this is truly where the work emerges). So, take inventory and ask yourself as sort of a mental checklist: have you intentionally designed your...

- audience experience?
- slide deck?
- technology and setting?
- content?
- delivery?
- growth and development?
- participation?

If so, we think you are well on your way to being a more effective presenter. And while that's great for you as an individual, perhaps more importantly, your message will have a better chance of truly making a difference. And that's the image we want in your mind as you think about your future self.

You are that person with a beautifully curated space, mastery of the technology, a well-structured outline, a beautiful and engaging slide deck, an inspirational and confident delivery, and participants who were active, engaged, and energized at the end of your presentation.

For us, that's the ultimate objective. And while we will never achieve perfection on any of the above-mentioned aspects, intentional design and deliberate practice will accelerate your progress. We believe that these skills will positively impact your career—and potentially, your organization, movement, or cause as well. This notion is the one that excites us about your experience with this book, and the growth we believe you can achieve because of it. If collectively, we can rid the world of long, boring, soul-sucking presentations, we will have made the world a better place together.

CONCLUSION

To conclude, we would like to say thank you! You are reading this sentence, which means you are committed to your personal development. Good work. As you continue to explore this emerging space of presenting online, we encourage you to reach out and help us learn more about what you are experiencing, as well as what worked for you and what was challenging. Scott can be reached at scott@captovation.ai, and you can contact Maria at maria@captovation.ai. Whether you want to share a resource we should include in the next edition, a potential topic for the future, or a piece of research you found valuable, we want to hear from you.

◆◆◆

"The passion for stretching yourself and sticking to it, even (or especially) when it's not going well, is the hallmark of the growth mindset. This is the mindset that allows people to thrive during some of the most challenging times in their lives."
—Carol Dweck, *Mindset*

Appendix—Navigating Nerves

Most interventions with a goal of minimizing public speaking anxiety are behavioral (e.g., they focus on the psychology of the individual) or pedagogic (e.g., they focus on skill development).[77] While some people can address the issue of nerves on their own, others might benefit from working with a professional to get to the source of the nerves to make lasting change. A cognitive behavioral therapist can help you better understand the psychological and physiological reactions you have either before or when presenting. Although we have listed 100 techniques for navigating nerves, the reality is that for each of you, it will be a different combination that works. For some, positive self-talk combined with double-checking your technology just might do the trick. For others, not so much. For Scott, deep breathing and visualizing never really made a distinct difference, but touchstones, letting go of perfection, early audience engagement, and playing the right music ahead of time really helped him manage nerves. We suggest picking one or some combination of techniques and running some experiments. The reality is that it will be a different combination for each of you. And, it will take some time to find the right mix.

Be patient with yourself; the fact that you are even reading this book says a lot about you! Whether you have chosen to or this book has been required or recommended, you are actively working to improve. As you read the list of strategies below, we encourage you to identify and write down 5–10 that sound realistic for you.

1. Positive self-talk. Place a sticky note with a positive reminder next to your computer.
2. Keep the temperature cool or warm in your presentation space. It depends on you!
3. See a therapist and talk about the source of your anxiety.
4. Join Toastmasters or a similar organization and practice presenting.
5. Ask a seasoned colleague to mentor you and provide feedback.
6. Ask your organization to hire a presentation coach.
7. Take a presentation skills course in the community, or teach a presentation skills course in your organization.
8. Use technology to plan, and use the results to help you track your anxiety (e.g., Captovation).
9. Practice the presentation and ask a colleague for feedback. As

scholar Chris Ireland suggests, "The lower the level of mastery, the greater the level of apprehension is likely to be."[78]
10. Incorporate appropriate humor and win the audience over early. Design for humor in a couple places
11. Begin with a fun activity like **Point North**[79] or **Changing Perspective**.[80]
12. Ask people to answer a question in the chat beforehand (e.g., first concert, favorite show growing up).
13. Practice the technology platform you will be using days in advance.
14. Design short breaks for yourself by showing a video or placing the audience in a discussion.
15. Be proud of yourself—honor that. You are putting yourself out there with this presentation, and that can be scary!
16. Arrive online 30 minutes early and test *everything*.
17. Build relationships before you begin, perhaps by networking with people who arrive early—e.g., ask "Carl, what is your role at XYZ Corp?"
18. Dress in a way that makes you feel confident. In other words, dress the part.
19. Tailor the talk to your audience in some meaningful way.
20. Use a touchstone to ground yourself; perhaps that is a small keepsake, an important piece jewelry, or something with meaning. Place it next to your computer (or if it's jewelry, incorporate it into your outfit).
21. Design your setting. Invest a little time and money to ensure it's an ideal environment for you.
22. Compliment an audience member on their setting or background.
23. Start your day in the best possible way. Perhaps it's a long walk, yoga, workout, a meditation, or even a better breakfast than you normally have.[81]
24. Focus on the larger meaning and purpose of your talk. Tap into your energy and enthusiasm for the topic.
25. Let go of perfection. The presentation will not be perfect, *and that's ok*.
26. Give yourself the credit you deserve for taking the spotlight and giving this presentation. This is a win in and of itself.
27. Say "who cares"—do not let the presentation get bigger in your head than it deserves to be.

28. Remain focused on the audience experience and be confident that you add value.
29. Build a slide deck that *you* are excited to share.
30. Avoid caffeine, or drink caffeine! It all depends on you.
31. Celebrate and honor your wins, no matter how small. This is a process and will take time.
32. Explore EMDR Therapy,[82] Cognitive Behavioral Therapy,[83] or Emotional Freedom Technique[84] as techniques to relieve anxiety.
33. Talk with loved ones before the presentation.
34. Be sure you are hydrated, and have a glass of water nearby, even if you don't need it. That glass of water could become a good excuse for a pause.
35. Get plenty of sleep.
36. Scenario-plan. Have a "Plan B" if you experience issues with Wi-Fi, and so forth.
37. Visualize success and imagine how proud you will be when the presentation is complete.
38. Design your presentations in a way that gives you a few breaks. Use the chat, a poll, or a video as an opportunity for a breather.
39. Unless it's a requirement, do not memorize your talk. Doing so places a large cognitive burden on yourself. Know the outline and then speak to the outline.
40. Do not put too much text on the slide. The slides will be easier to deliver well.
41. Do not have too much content on slides (e.g., multiple images, multiple graphs). If you can't figure out how you are going to get through a slide, that's an indicator that there is too much on there.
42. Authentically tap into your emotions around the importance of your topic.
43. Avoid throwaway comments like "I am so nervous."
44. For some, it's best to not "over-practice" or fixate on the talk.
45. Plant some allies in the audience who are on your side.
46. Scenario-plan for questions you may receive.
47. Scenario-plan for the detractors and build it into your presentation.
48. Don't overly focus on who's online, or who is not visible on video.
49. Take a deep breath and begin strong.
50. Imagine yourself playing the lead role in the (fictitious) award-winning film *The Confident Presenter* (bonus if you give yourself an Oscar afterward!).

51. Don't take yourself too seriously. Be professional, but be accessible. No one wants perfection.
52. Run your outline by some trusted advisors to ensure you've hit the high points.
53. Get the audience involved early through a question, poll, chat, or activity.
54. Be aware of your nervous tics ahead of time and try to minimize them (e.g., rocking/swaying, clicking a pen, talking too fast, playing with hair, touching your face, and fidgeting).
55. When you make a mistake, react with confidence, make a joke, use self-deprecating humor, or ignore it.
56. Eat a healthy meal before your talk.[85]
57. Plan a celebration for after the presentation.
58. Invite loved ones, mentors, or others to sign on (if that is appropriate).
59. Ensure a measured pace so you do not get ahead of yourself.
60. Say "yes" every time you are asked to present.
61. Don't finish the slide deck at the last minute. Work on it in small chunks weeks in advance and have the final (or close to it) ready to go at least a few days early so you can go through it multiple times.
62. Talk through your feelings with a loved one who can help you process your feelings.
63. Ask your kids how they handle feeling nervous and use their advice (within reason!).
64. Review your notes and presentation before you go to bed the night preceding your presentation, and again first thing in the morning the day of.
65. Minimize distractions to the best of your ability (e.g., pets, children, phones).
66. In addition to seeking feedback from a trusted advisor *before* the formal presentation, as for it after as well.
67. Include images in your slides that will elicit your enthusiasm and excitement.
68. Include a story that you are passionate about and are truly excited to share with others.
69. If you are in a flight of different presenters, ask if you can go first.
70. Play a certain song that "pumps you up" or "calms you down" as participants enter the online room—for Scott, it's Chris Joss's "Tune Down," and for Maria, it's John Mayer's "Waiting on the World to Change."

71. Build in a video that you know will elicit an emotional response.
72. Conduct research online about nerves, their sources, and build your own list of ideas.
73. Get mad at the "negative voice." It's holding you back from being awesome, so use your anger to work past it.
74. Let go of trying to please everyone. You won't—at least most of the time.
75. Write the biography of your nerves and anxiety around presenting. Tell the story and be as explicit as possible—what happens psychologically (e.g., negative self-talk) and physiologically (sweaty palms, shaky voice, increased pace, shaky hands, the red splotch, flushing)?
76. Purchase your own technology products and devices.
77. Have everything backed up on a jump or a cloud drive. Send the presentation to your contact ahead of time.
78. If possible, clear your day from stressful situations or trigger events.
79. Practice pieces of content with colleagues (i.e., practice administering a poll or incorporating the chat function).
80. Set a final one-on-one with your contact a day ahead of time to ensure all the details are set.
81. Identify a meditation, quote, or mantra that keeps you centered. Place this next to your computer.
82. Eliminate animations and extra steps in your slides. Make it as clean and simple as possible.
83. Use a simple structure that will help you stay on target, not lose your spot, and remain focused.
84. Don't drink alcohol, take beta blockers, or other drugs to calm your nerves.
85. Keep a timer near you so you are aware of time during the session.
86. Smile. Although you cannot see them, many will smile back.
87. Hug a loved one or pet before you go live.
88. Use Captovation to review the analytics after you've finished, and make a plan for next time.
89. Explore the work of Albert Bandura on developing self-efficacy.
90. Keep notes next to your computer. These could be points of emphasis, specific numbers, data, etc.
91. Visualize yourself as a confident speaker. This is your future. Keep this future self top of mind—a confident person sharing their expertise with people all over the globe.

APPENDIX

92. Print out a copy of your slides (we usually do either two or three per page) so you glance at what is coming next.
93. Reframe the adrenaline from anxiety to fuel.
94. Partner with a colleague or friend on the presentation to lessen the pressure and encourage collaboration and idea-sharing.
95. As people enter the virtual room, remember that you are "on." Smile, talk with participants, engage with your host, and so forth.
96. Visualize how you will feel after a wonderful presentation!
97. Fill your environment with pictures, books, artwork, and personal artifacts that make you feel confident.
98. Remember the key word that we presented you with at the beginning of this book to help you always maintain a growth mindset: "...yet."
99. Focus on your message and not the characteristics of the audience.[86]
100. While we do not suggest reading your notes, have them nearby in case you need them.

[1] Dweck, C. S. (2008). *Mindset: The new psychology of success.* Random House Digital, Inc.

[2] Dweck, C. (2014, September). *The power of believing that you can improve* [video]. TED Conferences. https://www.ted.com/talks/carol_dweck_the_power_of_believing_that_you_can_improve

[3] Joe, J., Kitchen, C., Chen, L., & Feng, G. (2015). A prototype public speaking skills assessment: An evaluation of human-scoring quality. *ETS Research Report Series, 2015*(2), 1–21.

[4] Nordquist, R. (2019). *Effective rhetorical strategies of repetition.* Retrieved from https://www.thoughtco.com/effective-strategies-ofrepetition-1691853.

[5] Sousa, D. A. (2006). *How the brain learns.* 3rd ed. Thousand Oaks, SAGE.

[6] Bunce, D. M., Flens, E. A., & Neiles, K. Y. (2010). How long can students pay attention in class? A study of student attention decline usingclickers. *Journal of Chemical Education, 87*(12), 1438–1443.

[7] Bradbury, N. A. (2016). Attention span during lectures: 8 seconds, 10 minutes, or more? *Advances in Physiology Education, 40,* 509–513.

[8] Bolger, M. *Changing Perspective.* The Safe Zone Project. https://thesafezoneproject.com/activities/changing-perspective/

[9] Reece, R. (2012, May 6). *Management, Leadership, & Followership.* YouTube. https://www.youtube.com/watch?v=OWMH_vXm-5BY&t=9s

[10] Pinker, S. (2018, June.) *Is the world getting better or worse? A look at the numbers* [Video]. TED. https://www.ted.com/talks/steven_pinker_is_the_world_getting_better_or_worse_a_look_at_the_numbers

[11] Pinker, S. (2018, May 21). *Is the world getting better or worse? A look at the numbers* [video]. TED. https://www.ted.com/talks/steven_pinker_is_the_world_getting_better_or_worse_a_look_at_the_numbers.

[12] Sinclair, D. A., & LaPlante, M. D. (2019). *Lifespan: Why we age—and why we don't have to.* Atria Books.

[13] SmarterEveryDay (2015, April 24). *The Backwards Brain Bicycle - Smarter Every Day 133.* YouTube. https://www.youtube.com/watch?v=MFzDaBzBlL0

[14] Cleveland Clinic (2013, February 127). *Empathy: The Human Connection to Patient Care.* You Tube. https://www.youtube.com/watch?v=cDDWvj_q-o8&t=18s

[15] Brownstein, J. (2009, October 1). *Most babies born today may live past 100.* ABC News. https://abcnews.go.com/Health/WellnessNews/half-todays-babiesexpected-live-past-100/story?id=8724273

[16] Janse, B. (2019, January 16). *Minto pyramid principle.* https://www.toolshero.com/communication-skills/minto-pyramid-principle/

[17] Minto, B. (1996). *The Minto pyramid principle.* Minto International Inc.

[18] Mahin, L. (2004). PowerPoint pedagogy. *Business Communication Quarterly, 67,* 219–222.

[19] Tufte, E. (2003). *The cognitive style of PowerPoint.* Cheshire, CT: Graphics Press.

[20] Luzardo, G., Guamán, B., Chiluiza, K., Castells, J., & Ochoa, X. (2014, November). Estimation of presentations skills based on slides and audio features. In *Proceedings of the 2014 ACM workshop on multimodal learning analytics workshop and grand challenge, 41.*

[21] Cornwell, L. (2017). *What is the impact of PowerPoint lectures on learning? A brief review of research.* http://www.hagerstownccc.edu/sites/default/files/documents/14-fletcher-powerpoint-research-review.pdf

[22] Marshall, M. (2012, June). *Talk nerdy to me* [Video]. TED. https://www.ted.com/talks/melissa_marshall_talk_nerdy_to_me

[23] Garner, J. K. & Alley, M. (2013). How the design of presentation slides affects audience comprehension: A case for the assertion-evidence approach. *International Journal of Engineering Education, 29*(6), 1577.

[24] Duarte, N. (2008). *Slide:ology: The art and science of creating great presentations* (Vol. 1). Sebastapol, CA: O'Reilly Media.

[25] Reynolds, G. (2011). *Presentation Zen: Simple ideas on presentation design and delivery.* New Riders.

[26] Toufani, A. (2017, July 21). *Exonomics* [video]. https://www.youtube.com/watch?v=jwKztTXdlkQ&t=405s

[27] Dowd, M. (2020, April 7). How to look good on camera according to Tom Ford. *New York Times.* https://www.nytimes.com/2020/04/07/style/tom-ford-video-chat-tips.html

[28] Hasan, S. A., Subhani, M. I., & Osman, M. (2011). New article of clothing translates the mood of an individual. *International Journal of Business and Social Sciences, 2*(23), 183–185.

[29] Laskey, J. (2020, March 25). How to look your best on a webcam. *New York Times.* https://www.nytimes.com/2020/03/25/realestate/coronavirus-webcam-appearance.html

[30] Goman, C. K. (2020, May 3). Body language hacks to project leadership presence on Zoom. *Forbes.* https://www.forbes.com/sites/carolkinseygoman/2020/05/03/body-language-hacks-to-project-leadership-presence-on-zoom/?sh=cd9d6bb4833d

[31] Chen, B. (2020, March 25). The dos and don'ts of online video meetings. *New York Times.* https://www.nytimes.com/2020/03/25/technology/personaltech/online-video-meetings-etiquette-virus.html

[32] Buzarin, I. (2020). *How to prep for speaking at a virtual conference. Medium.* https://medium.com/shiftconf/how-to-prep-for-speaking-at-a-virtualconference-2bb4ecfc0d30

[33] Bar, M., Neta, M., & Linz, H. (2006). Very first impressions. *Emotion, 6*(2), 269–278.

[34] Willis, J., & Todorov, A. (2006). First impressions: Making up your mind after a 100-ms exposure to a face. *Psychological Science, 17*(7), 592–598.

[35] Hartman, J. L., & LeMay, E. (2004). Managing presentation anxiety. *Delta Pi Epsilon Journal, 46*(3).

FOOTNOTES

[36] Ross (2014, June 18). *Brain games–Duchenne* Smile [Video]. Youtube. https://www.youtube.com/watch?v=ZxgCpyOAqGI

[37] Enge, N., & Enge, M. (2018). *The science of speaking*. Cioppino Press.

[38] Laserna, C. M., Seih, Y. T., & Pennebaker, J. W. (2014). Um...who like says you know: Filler word use as a function of age, gender, and personality. *Journal of Language and Social Psychology, 33*(3), 328–338.

[39] Brennan, S. E., & Williams, M. (1995). The feeling of another's knowing: Prosody and filled pauses as cues to listeners about the metacognitive states of speakers. *Journal of Memory and Language, 34*(3), 383–398.

[40] Duvall, E. D., Robbins, A. S., Graham, T. R., & Divett, S. (2014). Exploring filler words and their impact. *Schwa. Language & Linguistics, 11*, 44.

[41] Montes, C. C., Heinicke, M. R., & Geierman, D. M. (2019). Awareness training reduces college students' speech disfluencies in public speaking. *Journal of Applied Behavior Analysis, 52*(3), 746–755.

[42] Robbins, T. (2006, February). *Why we do what we do* [Video]. TED. https:// www.ted.com/talks/tony_robbins_why_we_do_what_we_do

[43] Treasure, J. (2013, June). *How to speak so that people want to listen* [Video]. TED. https://www.ted.com/talks/julian_treasure_how_to_speak_so_that_people_want_to_listen

[44] Haider, F., Cerrato, L., Campbell, N., & Luz, S. (2016, March). Presentation quality assessment using acoustic information and hand movements in *2016 IEEE International Conference on Acoustics, Speech and Signal Processing (ICASSP)*, 2812–2816

[45] Beebe, S. A., & Biggers, T. (1988, June). Emotion-eliciting qualities of speech delivery and their effect on credibility and comprehension. Paper presented at the Annual Meeting of the International Communication Association, New Orleans, LA.

[46] Dupuis, K., & Pichora-Fuller, M. K. (2010). Use of affective prosody by young and older adults. *Psychology and Aging, 25*(1), 16.

[47] Toastmasters International (2011). *Your speaking voice: Tips for adding strength and authority to your voice*. https://toastmaster-scdn.azureedgenet/medias/files/department-documents/education-documents/199-your-speaking-voice.pdf

[48] Gallo, C. (2014). *Talk like TED: the 9 public-speaking secrets of the world's top minds*. St. Martin's Press.

[49] Anderson, C. (2016). *TED talks: The official TED guide to public speaking*. Houghton Mifflin Harcourt.

[50] Enge, N., & Enge, M. (2018*). The science of speaking*. Cioppino Press.

[51] Miller, J. L., Grosjean, P., & Lomanto, C. (1984). Articulation rate and its variability in spontaneous speech: A reanalysis and some implications. *Phonetica, 41*, 216–225.

[52] Stine, E. A. L., Wingfield, A., & Myers, S. D. (1990). Age differences in processing information from television news: The effects of bisensory augmentation. *Journal of Gerontology: Psychological Sciences, 45*, 1–8.

[53] Gordon, M. S., Daneman, M., & Schneider, B. A. (2009). Comprehension of speeded discourse by younger and older listeners. *Experimental Aging Research, 35*(3), 277–296.

[54] Treasure, J. (2013, June). *How to speak so that people want to listen* [Video]. TED. https://www.ted.com/talks/

[55] MacGregor, L. J., Corley, M., & Donaldson, D. I. (2010). Listening to the sound of silence: Disfluent silent pauses in speech have consequences for listeners. *Neuropsychologia, 48*(14), 3982–3992.

[56] MacGregor, L. J., Corley, M., & Donaldson, D. I. (2010). Listening to the sound of silence: Disfluent silent pauses in speech have consequences for listeners. *Neuropsychologia, 48*(14), 3982–3992.

[57] Woolbert, C. H. (1920). Effects of various modes of public reading. *Journal of Applied Psychology, 4*(2-3), 162.

[58] Saukh, O., & Maag, B. (2019, April). Quantle: Fair and honest presentation coach in your pocket. In *Proceedings of the 18th International Conference on Information Processing in Sensor Networks*, 253–264.

[59] Scherer, K. R., London, H., & Wolf, J. J. (1973). The voice of confidence: Paralinguistic cues and audience evaluation. *Journal of Research in Personality, 7*(1), 31–44.

[60] Haider, F., Cerrato, L., Campbell, N., & Luz, S. (2016, March). Presentation quality assessment using acoustic information and hand movements. In *2016 IEEE International Conference on Acoustics, Speech and Signal Processing (ICASSP)*, 2812–2816.

[61] Rosenshine, B. (1970). Enthusiastic teaching: A research review. *The School Review, 78*(4), 499–514.

[62] Hincks, R. (2004). Processing the prosody of oral presentations. In *InSTIL/ICALL Symposium 2004*.

[63] Singhal, A., Ali, M. R., Baten, R. A., Kurumada, C., Marvin, E. W., & Hoque, M.E. (2018, May). Analyzing the impact of gender on the automationof feedback for public speaking. In *2018 13th IEEE International Conference on Automatic Face & Gesture Recognition (FG 2018)*, 607–613.

[64] Das, S., Gandhi, N., Naik, T., & Shilkrot, R. (2019, May). Increase apparent public speaking fluency by speech augmentation. In *ICASSP 2019-2019 IEEE International Conference on Acoustics, Speech and Signal Processing (ICASSP)*, 6890–6894.

[65] Kelleher, K. (2017, November 17). *Vocal Fry & Upspeak* [Video]. Pecha Kucha Nashville. https://www.youtube.com/watch?v=k8s_voON1ws

[66] Gross, T. (2015, July 23). From upspeak to vocal fry: Are we 'policing' young women's voices? [Audio podcast]. https://www.npr.org/transcripts/425608745?storyId=425608745

[67] Gross, T. (2015, July 23). From upspeak to vocal fry: Are we 'policing' young women's voices? [Audio podcast]. https://www.npr.org/transcripts/425608745?storyId=425608745

[68] Iverson, J. M., & Goldin-Meadow, S. (1998). Why people gesture when they speak. *Nature, 396*(6708), 228.

[69] Beattie, G., & Shovelton, H. (1999). Do iconic hand gestures really contribute anything to the semantic information conveyed by speech? An experimental investigation. *Semiotica, 123*(1–2), 1–30.

[70] Hubbard, A. L., Wilson, S. M., Callan, D. E., & Dapretto, M. (2009). Giving speech a hand: Gesture modulates activity in auditory cortex during speech perception. *Human Brain Mapping, 30*(3), 1029.

[71] Skipper, J. I., Goldin-Meadow, S., Nusbaum, H. C., & Small, S. L. (2009). Gestures orchestrate brain networks for language understanding. *Current Biology, 19*(8), 661–667.

[72] Toastmasters International. (2016). *Using body language*. https://www.toastmasters.org/resources/using-body-language.

[73] Van Edwards, V. *5 secrets of a successful TED Talk*. https://www.scienceofpeople.com/secrets-of-a-successful-ted-talk/

[74] Csabai, M. (2015, November 25). *4 stages of learning anything*. https://mindinmotion.co.za/4-stages-of-learning-anything/

[75] Ericsson, A., & Pool, R. (2016). *Peak: Secrets from the new science of expertise*. Houghton Mifflin Harcourt.

[76] Muther, C., & Teitell, B. (2020, March 23). The 12 most annoying co-workers you face on Zoom. https://www.bostonglobe.com/2020/03/23/lifestyle/12-most-annoying-co-workers-you-face-zoom/

[77] Ireland, C. (2016). Student oral presentations: Developing the skills and reducing the apprehension. IATED, 1474–1483.

[78] Ireland, C. (2020). Apprehension felt towards delivering oral presentations: A case study of accountancy students. *Accounting Education, 29*(3), 305–320.

[79] Reece, R. (2012, May 6). *Management, Leadership, & Followership*. YouTube. https://www.youtube.com/watch?v=OWMH_vXm-5BY&t=9s

[80] Bolger, M. *Changing Perspective*. The Safe Zone Project. https://thesafezoneproject.com/activities/changing-perspective/

[81] Morgan, N. (2008). How to become an authentic speaker. *Harvard Business Review, 11*(86), 115–119.

[82] Barker, R. T., & Barker, S. B. (2007). The use of EMDR in reducing presentation anxiety. *Journal of EMDR Practice and Research, 1*(2), 100–108.

[83] Bubel, M., Jiang, R., Lee, C. H., Shi, W., & Tse, A. (2016, May). AwareMe: Addressing fear of public speech through awareness. In *Proceedings of the 2016 CHI Conference Extended Abstracts on Human Factors in Computing Systems*, 68–73.

[84] Boath, L. (2012). Tapping for PEAS: Emotional freedom technique (EFT) in reducing presentation expression anxiety syndrome (PEAS) in university students. *Innovative Practice in Higher Education, 1*(2).

[85] Morgan, N. (2008). *How to become an authentic speaker*. Harvard Business Review, 11(86), 115–119.

[86] Ireland, C. J. (2018). *Reducing public speaking anxiety in undergraduates: A case study of an intervention with accountancy students* [Doctoral dissertation, University of Huddersfield]. British Library EThOS.

FOOTNOTES

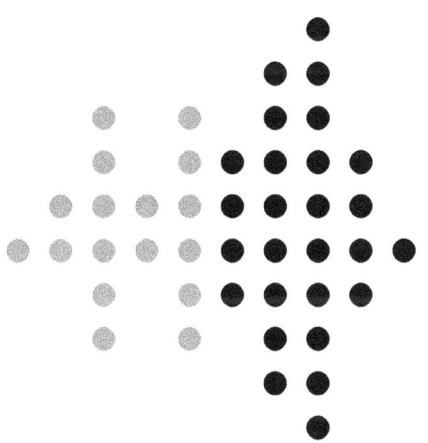

About the Authors

Scott J. Allen, Ph.D.

Scott J. Allen, Ph.D. is the Standard Products—Dr. James S. Reid Chair in Management at John Carroll University. Allen is an associate professor and teaches courses in leadership, management skills, and executive communication. He's received awards for his teaching and his primary stream of research focuses on leadership development and he's published more than 50 book chapters and peer-reviewed journal articles. His most recent project is a textbook for Sage—*Discovering Leadership: Designing Your Success* (2019). Scott is also the host of the podcast—*Phronesis: Practical Wisdom for Leaders*. In addition to writing and speaking, Scott consults, facilitates workshops, and leads retreats across industries and serves as the chair and co-founder of the Collegiate Leadership Competition. Scott has served on the board of the International Leadership Association, Association of Leadership Educators, and OBTS Teaching Society for Management Educators. To learn more about Scott, visit www.scottjallen.net.

ABOUT THE AUTHORS

Maria Soriano Young, M.A.

Maria is a Communication Manager for the Chair of the Heart, Vascular, & Thoracic Institute at Cleveland Clinic. She is also a freelance editor who has worked across a number of industries. Her background includes 11 years in higher education; she taught a variety of courses at John Carroll University, including business communication and first-year writing, directed the Writing Center, and coached graduate assistants to become effective teachers. She has presented at numerous conferences throughout her career, and has also published on various topics in the field of composition and rhetoric.

Praise for Captovation

Online Presentations by Design offers a timely guidebook that will elevate your online presentation skills. Whether you're a senior executive or an employee with high potential looking to set yourself apart, you will gain new and useful skills from this text, from planning your presentation to delivering your deck.

—Marshall Goldsmith is the New York Times #1 bestselling author of *Triggers*, *Mojo*, and *What Got You Here Won't Get You There* and Thinkers 50 #1 Executive Coach.

Scott Allen and Maria Soriano Young have created an exceptionally comprehensive resource for instructors, students, savvy executives, and anyone who seeks to make memorable online presentations. Just long enough to be helpful without overwhelming, *Captovation* focuses on the design of slide decks, principles of delivery, and control of environment—all adapted to the new norms of presenting in an online setting. Well-researched and beautifully written, this is a must-have for anyone unsure of how to craft, revise, and deliver presentations with the new online medium.

—Dr. Mary Ellen Guffey, world's leading business communication textbook author

The game is played differently online and this is the winning playbook. Either absorb the fundamentals of the sport or keep missing opportunities to win.

—Gordon Daily, CEO & Co-Founder at BoxCast, Inc.

PRAISE FOR CAPTOVATION

As presentation is one of the key elements of our work in the Center for Career Services at JCU, this book has solidified some of the "must-haves" and "dos and dont's" to create an effective and concise presentation for our various audiences with details on mindset, slide design, setting, delivery, and audience engagement. Each chapter provides a framework for a successful presentation experience that will be relevant in all presentation environments.

—Abby McNutt, MBA Candidate

◆◆◆

In *Captovation*, Scott Allen and Maria Soriano Young pull back the curtain to reveal not only what to think but also how to think about designing superior online presentations. This straightforward resource allows the presenter to unlock skills and narrow in on what's most important. Whether you're a student, coach, or regularly give presentations for work, *Captovation* offers you significant insight into the differences between online and in-person presentations and will ensure your presentation is engaging and memorable.

—Ken Kasee, Speech and Debate Coach of 2019 National Champions Maggie Mills and Sasha Haines

◆◆◆

Captovation: Online Presentations by Design is the essential guide for presenters planning engrossing and engaging online presentations. Many of the principles and concepts enunciated in the book go beyond the scope of online presentations and apply equally to in-person presentations. This well-researched and erudite book is an indispensable addition to the bookshelves of presenters and participants alike.

—Deepak Menon, DTM, 2019-2020 Toastmasters International President

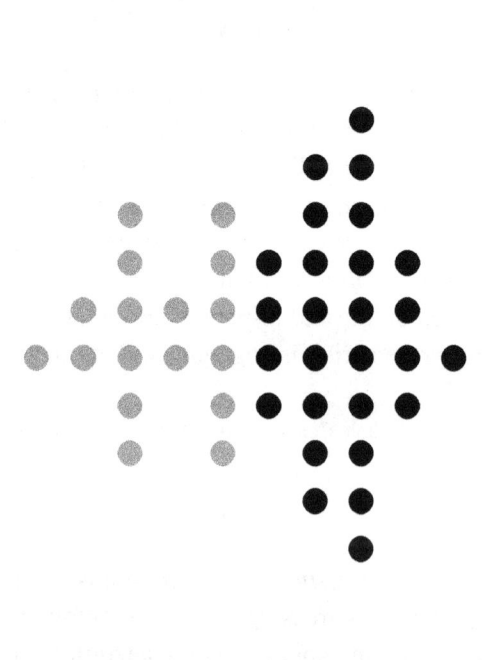

www.ingramcontent.com/pod-product-compliance
Lightning Source LLC
LaVergne TN
LVHW090116080426
835507LV00040B/907